30-minute
Vegetarian

 A Pyramid Cookery Paperback

30-minute
Vegetarian

Joanna Farrow

Photography by William Reavell

hamlyn

An Hachette Livre UK Company
www.hachettelivre.co.uk

A Pyramid Paperback

First published in Great Britain in 1998 by Hamlyn,
a division of Octopus Publishing Group Ltd
2–4 Heron Quays, London E14 4JP
www.octopusbooksusa.com

Revised edition published 2004

This edition published 2009

Copyright © Octopus Publishing Group Ltd 2004,
2008, 2009

Distributed in the U.S. and Canada by Octopus
Books USA:
c/o Hachette Book Group USA
237 Park Avenue
New York NY 10017

This material was previously published as
30-Minute Vegetarian

Joanna Farrow asserts the moral right to be
identified as the author of this work

ISBN 978-0-600-61958-1

A CIP catalog record for this book is available from
the British Library

Printed and bound in China

10 9 8 7 6 5 4 3 2 1

NOTES
1 The Food and Drug Administration advises that
eggs should not be consumed raw. It is prudent
for more vulnerable people such as pregnant and
nursing mothers, invalids, the elderly, babies, and
young children to avoid uncooked or lightly cooked
dishes made with eggs.

2 This book includes dishes made with nuts and
nut derivatives. It is advisable for those with
known allergic reactions to nuts and nut
derivatives and those who may be potentially
vulnerable to these allergies, such as pregnant
and nursing mothers, invalids, the elderly, babies,
and children, to avoid dishes made with nuts and
nut oils. It is also prudent to check the labels of
pre-prepared ingredients for the possible inclusion
of nut derivatives.

contents

introduction

This book will appeal to anyone who knows how exotic and exciting contemporary vegetarian cooking can be.

Like many children of my generation, I was raised on a meat-based diet, but even then I found a traditional roast dinner or a classic winter stew rather difficult to swallow, despite my mother's evident cooking skills. I have memories of trying to hide unwanted pieces of beef or lamb under my knife and fork in the naive hope that my parents would not notice. This was possibly a taste of things to come for me personally, but maybe the reality is that most of us have moved away from the once-standard "meat and two veg" diet.

This is, of course, an inevitable consequence of the explosion of interest in all things relating to food. We travel more and seize the opportunity to sample different cuisines, new flavors, and ingredients that were completely alien to our parents. There is also now a far greater variety of foods widely available, gathered from all over the world. Television programs, food magazines, and cookbooks all fuel our desire to enjoy an ever-widening feast of interesting flavors.

All this has helped the vegetarian cause tremendously. Moral issues aside, people have discovered that there are many non-meat based cuisines around the globe from which to draw new inspiration, and so meat (like my mother's roasts) has been pushed to one side. How many people eat as much meat as they did even ten years ago?

My aim in this book is to show that vegetarian cooking has thrown off its dull yet worthy image, epitomized by the token vegetable lasagna or the equally dreary vegetarian alternatives that some restaurants used to (and still do in some cases) offer. Whether you are a confirmed vegetarian or seeking a fresh approach, here is a collection of recipes to excite and delight—a heady mix of stimulating flavors and diverse culinary practises. And it is all fast food! It takes very little time to whiz up a delicious homemade pesto and toss it with pasta, or to throw a blend of aromatic Far Eastern spices in a pan with beans and vegetables, then pile them onto noodles. This spontaneity captures the essence of fresh herbs and the pungency of spices to create imaginative, flavorful dishes in less than 30 mins. Yes, you might have to plan what you are going to cook a little more, and yes, it might mean using a few more ingredients, but it certainly will not involve you in spending hours in the kitchen assembling complicated or expensive creations.

For anyone who is yet to be convinced about the value of vegetarian cooking, think of your meat-based diet as a habit. Once you break the habit of meat-eating, it is not necessarily a case of giving up anything but opening yourself up to a wealth of new, vibrant and easy ways of cooking.

Joanna
Farrow

glossary

Arugula This is a delicious peppery-tasting salad leaf. Try growing your own rather than buying ridiculously expensive small supermarket packs. Sow some in a pot or in the garden monthly throughout the summer for a cheap and far more flavorful supply.

Balsamic vinegar This has been a popular ingredient for some years now, with a far richer, sweeter flavor than ordinary wine vinegars (although these still have their uses in many dishes). It is made in Modena, Italy, and is aged in wooden barrels for anything up to 50 years, the maturing time developing its flavor and price!

Cheeses Cheese plays an important role in vegetarian cooking, not purely as a flavoring but as a useful source of protein, calcium, and vitamins. While many vegetarians will eat non-vegetarian cheeses, others avoid it because of the presence of rennet used to solidify many cheeses. In recent years, there has been a huge increase in the number of cheeses produced using vegetarian rennet. The difference in taste is barely discernible and it behaves no differently when used in cooking.
Brie and Camembert: These are encased in a soft, white penicillin mold and vary considerably from dry and crumbly to runny and strongly flavored. Sliced, they can be lightly broiled and tossed with pasta or used as a topping for toast, pizzas, or pastries.
Haloumi: This firm, salty Greek cheese has a dense, chewy texture that is delicious broiled or fried and tossed into salads. It goes particularly well with fruit, such as grapes and pears.
Mascarpone: A deliciously soft, velvet-smooth cream cheese made with cows' milk. It is good

in savory dishes as it melts to create wonderfully rich sauces, as well as in sweet dishes as a creamy trifle or tiramisu base.
Mozzarella: A fresh, moist, subtle-flavored cheese, made from either buffalo or cows' milk. It has an inviting stringy quality when melted and is often combined with more intensely flavored cheeses, such as Parmesan, to add flavor. Excellent on pizzas or pastries, or in salads.
Parmesan: A strongly flavored hard, salty cheese which is matured for years to develop the full flavor. Always buy in a block rather than ready-grated. Leftovers can be grated and frozen.
Ricotta: A soft, bland, fresh cheese that is often stirred into pasta or used in pastry fillings. It also makes a very quick and easy dessert. Try mixing the cheese with chocolate, ginger, dried fruit, and liqueurs.

Chilies These vary considerably in heat intensity and unfortunately there is often no way of knowing how hot they are until you cook them. As a rough guide, the tiny Thai chilies, both red and green varieties, are always very fiery, while the larger, chubbier chilies, usually sold loose in supermarkets, tend to be milder. Sometimes more unusual chilies, such as Scotch Bonnet and Habañero, are available in small packs, usually labeled to show the heat intensity.

Coconut Once you have mastered the art of opening a fresh coconut, the grated flesh adds a refreshing, nutty flavor to salads and stir-fries. To open the coconut, first pierce the three "eyes" with a skewer (sometimes a corkscrew works well) and drain the juice into a beaker. Some people love this nutritious, opaque juice, while others hate it! Put the coconut in a strong plastic carrier bag and beat with a hammer to crack it into several pieces. Ease out the flesh from the shell.

Coconut milk
This is not the juice from inside the whole coconut, but a thick, velvety smooth, creamy milk that is processed from coconut flesh. Sold in cans and cartons, it is one of the most widely used cooking liquids in Southeast Asian and Caribbean cookery, and excellent for giving "body" and richness to vegetarian soups, stews, and oriental dishes.

Creamed coconut
Very concentrated in flavor, a small chunk (about 1–2 oz) can be added to soups, stews, and sauces to thicken and intensify flavor. Creamed coconut melts as it heats up.

Lemon grass
This is now widely available fresh and adds a wonderful, aromatic, lemony flavor to soups and spicy dishes. Peel away any tough, discolored leaves, then finely slice or chop the rest. If you cannot find fresh lemon grass, look for it dried in jars with the other spices.

Noodles
There are many different types of noodle available, from rice noodles to those made from wheat, bean starch, and buckwheat. Some are thick and ribbon-like, while others are fine like vermicelli. They generally cook very quickly and rice noodles will turn mushy and paste-like if overcooked.

Olive oil
Extra virgin olive oil comes from the first cold pressing of the olives, giving a rich flavor and deep color. Subsequent pressings produce oils of a lighter flavor. It is worth keeping an extra virgin olive oil for salad dressings and dishes in which you want an intense, Mediterranean flavor, and a lighter, cheaper one for other cooking and for frying.

You can easily make your own flavored oils by steeping sprigs of rosemary, tarragon, thyme, bay leaves, or some whole fresh chilies in the oil for a few weeks before using.

Pasta
This is a blend of flour and water, sometimes with the addition of egg. Fresh pasta has a better flavor and texture than dried and cooks very quickly, usually in less time than packet directions suggest, so take care when cooking. Leftover fresh pasta can be frozen successfully. Dried pasta makes a good storecupboard alternative but brands vary considerably in quality. When draining any cooked pasta, always leave the last of the cooking water clinging to the pasta, to prevent the dish from being dry.

Pesto
This is a blend of basil, pine nuts, Parmesan cheese, garlic, and oil which can be bought in jars or, preferably, homemade. Simply put a clove of chopped garlic, a handful of basil leaves, 3 tablespoons pine nuts, and ½ cup grated Parmesan cheese in a food processor or blender and process, gradually adding a little olive oil, to make a thick, oily paste. Pesto is delicious simply tossed with pasta for a quick and easy supper, or stirred into soups and sauces. Red pesto has tomatoes added to the basic recipe.

Sun-dried tomato pesto (see page 65) makes a delicious variation on the pesto theme.

Polenta
This is made from ground corn kernels and is cooked blended with water to make a thick paste. Serve it soft, rather like mashed potatoes, or spread it on a tray, leave to set, then slice for broiling or baking, preferably with a cheese topping. Its bland flavor can be enhanced by the addition of garlic, olive oil, herbs, saffron, or chilies. Buy packs labeled "instant polenta" which cooks much faster.

Rice
There are dozens of varieties available. Most cook quickly, making a useful alternative to pasta and potatoes, although some varieties of red, brown, and "wild" rice take much longer. For spicy dishes, choose white or

brown basmati rice or Thai fragrant rice, which has a softer, fluffier texture and better flavor than regular long-grain rice. Italian risotto rices, either arborio or carnaroli, are very popular for making classic, creamy risottos. Flavor with mushrooms, asparagus, or simply cheese for a quick and easy vegetarian meal.

Saffron
It is very expensive, but saffron adds a distinctive flavor and color to many dishes that no other spice can imitate. It is perfect for Mediterranean rice and bean dishes, or for adding to polenta and potatoes.

Sun-dried tomatoes
These intensely flavored dried tomatoes, usually bought in oil, are so useful in northern climates where ordinary tomatoes generally lack the color and sweet flavor of those grown around the Mediterranean. Chopped up, they are great for adding flavor intensity to tomato soups and vegetable stews. Sun-dried tomato paste is equally useful.

Tapenade
A paste-like blend of olives, garlic, capers, and olive oil that can be store-bought or made at home by simply blending 3 tablespoons capers, ⅔ cup pitted black olives, 6 tablespoons olive oil, and a little garlic, herbs, and seasoning. If buying, check that the brand does not contain anchovies.

Tofu
Made from soy beans and sold in block form, tofu is bland in both taste and appearance, but should not be disregarded. Its assets are its nutritional value as a meat replacement and its great versatility in vegetarian cooking. Use it as a "carrier" for strongly flavored ingredients such as soy sauce, garlic, ginger, lemon grass, and spices. It is also available smoked.

Silken tofu is a lighter version of regular tofu. Easy to mash or blend, it is generally used in drinks and as a dairy replacement in desserts.

Vegetable stock
A vital ingredient in vegetarian soups, stews, casseroles, rice, and vegetable dishes. Liquid stock concentrate, bought in small jars, has a better flavor than the reconstituted cubes for everyday vegetarian cooking. For special occasions, buy fresh vegetable stock or make your own if you have time. Use the vegetables listed below as a guide, but throw in any other leftover vegetable trimmings, such as cabbage, broccoli, zucchini, fennel, scallions, or celeriac. Both the color and flavor of homemade vegetable stock is rich and intense.

Makes 4 cups

2 tablespoons olive oil
1 large onion, chopped, plus skins
2 carrots, chopped
¼ lb turnip or parsnip
3 celery sticks, sliced
¼ lb mushrooms, sliced
2 bay leaves
several thyme and parsley sprigs
2 tomatoes, chopped
2 teaspoons black peppercorns

one Heat the oil in a large saucepan. Add the onion, carrots, turnip or parsnip, celery, and mushrooms, and fry gently for 5 mins. Add the herbs, tomatoes, peppercorns, and onion skins, and cover with 3¾ pints water.
two Bring to a boil, partially cover and simmer gently for 1 hour. Cool, then strain and refrigerate for up to 2 days.

soups

Soups are without doubt among the easiest, most comforting ways to enjoy vegetarian food. Generous portions thick with chunky vegetables or pulses and served with warm, grainy bread make really satisfying main-meal dishes, while smoothly blended, light, and fragrant versions whet the appetite for a delicious meal to follow.

green lentil soup with spiced butter

preparation time **7 mins**
cooking time **23 mins**
total time **30 mins** serves **4**

3 tablespoons olive oil
2 onions, sliced
2 bay leaves
¾ cup green lentils, rinsed
4 cups Vegetable Stock (see page 9)
½ teaspoon ground turmeric
small handful of cilantro, roughly chopped
salt and pepper

SPICED BUTTER
¼ cup lightly salted butter, softened
1 large garlic clove, crushed
1 teaspoon paprika
1 teaspoon cumin seeds
1 red chili, seeded and thinly sliced

one Heat the oil in a saucepan. Add the
onions and fry for 3 mins. Add the bay
leaves, lentils, stock, and turmeric. Bring
to a boil, then reduce the heat, cover and
simmer for 20 mins until the lentils are
tender and turning mushy.
two Meanwhile, to prepare the spiced
butter, beat the butter with the garlic,
paprika, cumin seeds, and chili, and transfer
to a small serving dish.
three Stir the cilantro into the soup and
season to taste with salt and pepper. Serve
with the spiced butter at the table for
stirring into the soup.

lima bean and sun-dried tomato soup

preparation time **5 mins**
cooking time **20 mins**
total time **25 mins** serves **4**

3 tablespoons olive oil
1 onion, finely chopped
2 celery sticks, thinly sliced
2 garlic cloves, thinly sliced
2 x 14 oz cans lima beans, rinsed and drained
4 tablespoons sun-dried tomato paste
3¾ cups Vegetable Stock (see page 9)
1 tablespoon chopped rosemary or thyme
salt and pepper
Parmesan cheese shavings, to serve

one Heat the oil in a saucepan. Add the
onion and fry for 3 mins until softened. Add
the celery and garlic, and fry for 2 mins.
two Add the lima beans, sun-dried tomato
paste, stock, rosemary or thyme, and a
little salt and pepper. Bring to a boil, then
reduce the heat, cover and simmer gently
for 15 mins. Serve sprinkled with the
Parmesan shavings.

Although it takes only a few minutes to prepare,
this chunky soup distinctly resembles a robust
Italian minestrone. It makes a worthy main course
served with bread and plenty of Parmesan cheese.

black bean soup with soba noodles

preparation time **5 mins**
cooking time **10 mins**
total time **15 mins** serves **4**

7 oz dried soba noodles
2 tablespoons peanut or vegetable oil
1 bunch of scallions, sliced
2 garlic cloves, roughly chopped
1 red chili, seeded and sliced
1½ inch piece of fresh ginger root, peeled
   and grated
½ cup black bean sauce or black bean
   stir-fry sauce
3 cups Vegetable Stock (see page 9)
1¾ cups shredded bok choy or spring greens
2 teaspoons soy sauce
1 teaspoon superfine sugar
⅓ cup raw, unsalted shelled peanuts

one Cook the noodles in plenty of boiling
water for about 5 mins until just tender.
two Meanwhile, heat the oil in a saucepan.
Add the scallions and garlic, and fry gently
for 1 min.
three Add the chili, ginger, black bean
sauce, and stock, and bring to a boil. Stir
in the bok choy or spring greens, soy sauce,
sugar, and peanuts. Reduce the heat and
simmer gently, uncovered, for 4 mins.
four Drain the noodles and pile into four
serving bowls. Ladle the soup over the
noodles and serve immediately.

new potato, cilantro, and leek soup

preparation time **5 mins**
cooking time **20 mins**
total time **25 mins** serves **4**

1 lb waxy new potatoes, such as Jersey Royals,
   scrubbed
3 small leeks, trimmed
3 tablespoons butter
1 tablespoon black mustard seeds
1 onion, chopped
1 garlic clove, thinly sliced
4 cups Vegetable Stock (see page 9)
plenty of freshly grated nutmeg
small handful of cilantro, roughly chopped
salt and pepper
warm bread, to serve

one Halve each potato, or cut into ½ inch
slices if large. Halve the leeks lengthwise,
then cut them across into thin shreds.
two Melt the butter in a heavy-based
saucepan. Add the mustard seeds, onion,
garlic, and potatoes, and fry gently for
5 mins. Add the stock and nutmeg, and
bring just to a boil. Reduce the heat, cover
and simmer gently for about 10 mins until
the potatoes are just tender.
three Stir in the leeks and cilantro, and cook
for 5 mins more. Season to taste with salt
and pepper and serve with warm bread.

Soba noodles, traditional in Japanese cooking, are made
of buckwheat and wholemeal flour, giving them a nutty
flavor without the dryness of many wholemeal pastas.

spinach and mushroom soup

preparation time **5 mins**
cooking time **20 mins**
total time **25 mins** serves **4**

¼ cup butter
1 tablespoon peanut or vegetable oil
1 onion, finely chopped
5 oz shiitake mushrooms
6 oz chestnut or cup mushrooms
2 garlic cloves, crushed
2 inch piece of fresh ginger root, peeled
    and grated
4 cups Vegetable Stock (see page 9)
½ lb baby spinach
plenty of freshly grated nutmeg
salt and pepper
croutons, to serve

one Melt the butter with the oil in a large
saucepan. Add the onion and fry for
5 mins. Add the mushrooms and garlic
and fry for 3 mins.
two Stir in the ginger and stock. Bring to
a boil, then reduce the heat, cover and
simmer gently for 10 mins.
three Add the spinach and nutmeg, and
simmer gently for 2 mins. Season to taste
with salt and pepper and serve scattered
with croutons.

creamed corn and potato soup

preparation time **5 mins**
cooking time **15 mins**
total time **20 mins** serves **4**

2 tablespoons olive oil
1 onion, chopped
2 celery sticks, thinly sliced
4 cups Vegetable Stock (see page 9)
¾ lb potatoes, diced
2 cups frozen corn
2 tablespoons chopped tarragon
plenty of freshly grated nutmeg
4 tablespoons heavy cream
salt and pepper

one Heat the oil in a large saucepan. Add
the onion and celery, and fry gently for
5 mins. Add the stock and bring to a boil.
two Add the potatoes, reduce the heat and
simmer, uncovered, for 5 mins. Add the corn
and tarragon, cover the pan and simmer for
5 mins more until the potatoes are tender.
three Transfer the soup to a food processor
or blender and process until pulpy but not
smooth, or leave the soup in the pan and
use a hand-held electric blender.
four Return the soup to the pan, if necessary,
and add the nutmeg and cream. Season to
taste with salt and pepper. Heat through
gently for 1 min before serving.

fresh ginger and parsnip soup

preparation time **5 mins**
cooking time **20 mins**
total time **25 mins** serves **4**

2 tablespoons butter
⅓ cup peeled and thinly sliced fresh ginger root
1 bunch of scallions
1 lb parsnips, sliced
4 cups Vegetable Stock (see page 9)
salt and pepper
crème fraîche, to serve

one Melt the butter in a saucepan. Add the ginger and fry gently for 1 min. Reserve 1 scallion. Roughly chop the remainder and add to the pan with the parsnips. Fry gently for 2 mins.

two Add the stock and bring to a boil. Reduce the heat, cover and simmer gently for 15 mins until the parsnips are tender. Meanwhile, shred the reserved scallion lengthwise into fine ribbons.

three Transfer the soup to a food processor or blender and process until smooth, or leave the soup in the pan and use a hand-held electric blender.

four Return the soup to the pan, if necessary. Season to taste with salt and pepper and heat through gently for 1 min, then ladle into soup bowls. Serve topped with a spoonful of crème fraîche scattered with scallion ribbons.

This is based on a Spanish soup in which the eggs are poached or oven-baked in a rich, garlicky broth. Here, pasta is added to give a little more substance to the dish.

garlic and paprika soup with a floating egg

preparation time **5 mins**
cooking time **15 mins**
total time **20 mins** serves **4**

4 tablespoons olive oil
12 thick slices of baguette (French bread)
5 garlic cloves, sliced
1 onion, finely chopped
1 tablespoon paprika
1 teaspoon ground cumin
good pinch of saffron threads
5 cups Vegetable Stock (see page 9)
¼ cup dried soup pasta
4 eggs
salt and pepper

one Heat the oil in a heavy-based saucepan. Add the bread and fry gently, turning once, until golden. Drain on paper towels.
two Add the garlic, onion, paprika, and cumin to the pan and fry gently for 3 mins. Add the saffron and stock and bring to a boil. Stir in the soup pasta. Reduce the heat, cover and simmer for about 8 mins until the pasta is just tender. Season to taste with salt and pepper.
three Break the eggs onto a saucer and slide into the pan one at a time. Cook for about 2 mins until poached.
four Stack 3 fried bread slices in each of 4 soup bowls. Ladle the soup over the bread, making sure each serving contains an egg. Serve immediately.

creamed shallot and rosemary soup

preparation time **10 mins**
cooking time **20 mins**
total time **30 mins** serves **4**

4 tablespoons olive oil
¾ lb shallots, sliced
1 red onion, roughly chopped
2 garlic cloves, roughly chopped
4 large rosemary sprigs
1 teaspoon superfine sugar
3 cups Vegetable Stock (see page 9)
5 tablespoons heavy cream
salt and pepper
toasted French bread croutons, to serve

one Heat the oil in a saucepan. Add the shallots, onion, garlic, rosemary, and sugar, and fry gently for about 5 mins until softened and lightly browned.
two Add the stock and bring to a boil. Reduce the heat, cover and simmer gently for about 15 mins until the shallots and onion are tender.
three Transfer the soup to a food processor or blender and process until smooth, or leave the soup in the pan and use a hand-held electric blender.
four Return the soup to the pan, if necessary. Stir in the cream and season to taste with salt and pepper. Heat through gently for 1 min, ladle into soup bowls, and serve sprinkled with croutons.

chili and pimiento soup

preparation time **10 mins**
cooking time **15 mins**
total time **25 mins** serves **4–6**

2 tablespoons olive oil
2 onions, chopped
2 garlic cloves, chopped
1 red chili, seeded and sliced
7 oz jar pimientos, drained
1 lb tomatoes, peeled
2 teaspoons superfine sugar
4 cups Vegetable Stock (see page 9)
2 tablespoons chopped cilantro
4 tablespoons crème fraîche
salt and pepper

one Heat the oil in a large saucepan. Add the onions, garlic, and chili and fry gently for 3 mins.
two Add the pimientos, tomatoes, sugar, and stock, and bring to a boil. Reduce the heat, cover and simmer gently for about 10 mins until the tomatoes are soft.
three Transfer the soup to a food processor or blender and process until smooth, or leave the soup in the pan and use a hand-held electric blender.
four Return the soup to the pan, if necessary, and stir in the cilantro and crème fraîche. Season to taste with salt and pepper, and heat through gently for 1 min before serving.

pumpkin and coconut soup

preparation time **5 mins**
cooking time **12 mins**
total time **17 mins** serves **4**

3 tablespoons peanut oil
4 thyme sprigs
2 garlic cloves, roughly chopped
1 red chili, seeded and roughly chopped
1 teaspoon cumin seeds
14 oz can solid-pack pumpkin
1 tablespoon dark muscovado sugar
1¾ cups Vegetable Stock (see page 9)
14 fl oz can coconut milk
1–2 tablespoons lemon or lime juice
salt and pepper
roughly chopped cilantro, to garnish

one Heat the oil in a saucepan. Strip the thyme leaves from the sprigs and add to the oil with the garlic, chili, and cumin seeds. Fry gently for 2 mins.
two Add the pumpkin, sugar, stock, and coconut milk, and bring to a boil. Reduce the heat, cover and simmer gently for 10 mins.
three Add the lemon or lime juice. Season to taste with salt and pepper, then serve scattered with the chopped cilantro.

zucchini and parmesan soup

preparation time **5 mins**
cooking time **15 mins**
total time **20 mins** serves **4**

2 tablespoons butter
1 tablespoon olive oil
1 large onion, chopped
1 lb zucchini, sliced
¾ cup pine nuts
1 tablespoon chopped sage
4 cups Vegetable Stock (see page 9)
1 cup crumbled Parmesan cheese
4 tablespoons heavy cream
salt and pepper

one Melt the butter with the oil in a large saucepan. Add the onion, zucchini, and pine nuts, and fry gently for about 5 mins until softened.

two Add the sage and stock, and bring to a boil. Reduce the heat, cover and simmer gently for 5 mins. Add the Parmesan cheese and cook for 2 mins.

three Transfer the soup to a food processor or blender and process lightly until the ingredients are partially blended but not smooth, or leave the soup in the pan and use a hand-held electric blender.

four Return the soup to the pan, if necessary, and stir in the cream and a little salt and pepper. Heat through gently for 1 min before serving.

pasta and noodles

The vast range of pasta and noodles available in supermarkets and specialist food stores is a bonus for all food lovers, particularly vegetarians. Opt for the more familiar Mediterranean approach with colorful vegetables and melting cheese or the exotic flavors of the East with egg noodle or rice noodle dishes.

cherry tomato and ricotta penne

preparation time **5 mins**
cooking time **10 mins**
total time **15 mins** serves **4**

10 oz dried penne
3 tablespoons olive oil
1 onion, chopped
4 garlic cloves, crushed
1 tablespoon chopped oregano
¾ lb cherry tomatoes, halved
1 teaspoon superfine sugar
3 tablespoons sun-dried tomato paste
½ lb ricotta cheese
salt and pepper

one Cook the pasta in plenty of lightly salted boiling water for about 10 mins or until just tender.

two Meanwhile, heat the oil in a frying pan. Add the onion and fry gently for 3 mins. Add the garlic, oregano, tomatoes, and sugar, and fry quickly for 1 min, stirring. Add the sun-dried tomato paste and 6 tablespoons of water. Season to taste with salt and pepper and bring to a boil. Put spoonfuls of the ricotta cheese into the pan and heat through gently for 1 min.

three Drain the pasta and pile onto serving plates. Spoon the tomato and cheese mixture on top, taking care not to break up the ricotta too much. Serve immediately.

ribbon pasta with eggplants and pine nuts

preparation time **5 mins**
cooking time **17 mins**
total time **22 mins** serves **4**

8 tablespoons olive oil
2 medium eggplants, diced
2 red onions, sliced
⅓ cup pine nuts
3 garlic cloves, crushed
5 tablespoons sun-dried tomato paste
⅔ cup Vegetable Stock (see page 9)
10 oz cracked pepper, tomato, or mushroom-
    flavored fresh ribbon pasta
¾ cup pitted black olives
salt and pepper
3 tablespoons roughly chopped Italian parsley,
    to garnish

one Heat the oil in a large frying pan or sauté pan, and fry the eggplants and onions for 8–10 mins until golden and tender. Add the pine nuts and garlic, and fry for 2 mins. Stir in the sun-dried tomato paste and stock, and cook for 2 mins.

two Meanwhile, cook the pasta in plenty of lightly salted boiling water for about 2 mins or until just tender.

three Drain the pasta and return to the pan. Add the sauce and olives. Season to taste with salt and pepper, and toss together over a moderate heat for 1 min until combined. Serve scattered with parsley.

pasta with watercress, dolcelatte, and walnut sauce

preparation time **5 mins**
cooking time **5 mins**
total time **10 mins** serves **4**

10 oz fresh pasta shapes or dried pasta
1 cup walnut pieces, toasted
6 oz mature Dolcelatte, diced
finely grated peel of 1 lemon
¾ cup crème fraîche
¼ lb watercress sprigs, coarse stalks removed
salt and pepper

one Cook the fresh pasta in plenty of lightly
salted boiling water for 2–3 mins until just
tender. Drain lightly and return to the pan
with the residual water still clinging to the
pasta. If you are using dried pasta, use the
same amount and cook it while you prepare
the other ingredients.
two Add the walnut pieces, cheese, lemon
peel, crème fraîche, and watercress, and
season to taste with salt and pepper.
three Toss the ingredients together over a
low heat for 2 mins until the crème fraîche
has melted to make a sauce and the
watercress has wilted. Serve immediately,
with a tangy tomato and red onion salad,
if desired.

ribbon pasta with tomatoes and tapenade

preparation time **10 mins**
cooking time **5 mins**
total time **15 mins** serves **4**

1 cup pitted black olives
1 red chili, seeded and sliced
4 tablespoons capers
2 tablespoons sun-dried tomato paste
3 tablespoons chopped basil
3 tablespoons chopped parsley or chervil
4 tomatoes, chopped
½ cup olive oil
¾ lb fresh ribbon pasta or fresh pasta shapes
salt and pepper
grated Parmesan cheese, to serve

one Put the olives, chili, and capers in a
food processor or blender and process until
quite finely chopped. Alternatively, finely
chop them by hand. Mix with the sun-dried
tomato paste, herbs, tomatoes, and oil.
Season to taste with salt and pepper.
two Cook the pasta in plenty of lightly
salted boiling water for 2–3 mins, or until
it is only just tender. Drain and return to
the saucepan.
three Add the olive mixture and toss the
ingredients together lightly over a low heat
for 2 mins. Transfer to serving plates and
serve sprinkled with Parmesan.

mushroom, zucchini, and mascarpone lasagna

preparation time **10 mins**
cooking time **20 mins**
total time **30 mins** serves **4**

⅓ cup dried bolete mushrooms
3 tablespoons olive oil
¼ lb fresh lasagna sheets, halved
½ lb mascarpone
2 garlic cloves, crushed
3 tablespoons chopped dill or tarragon
2 tablespoons butter
1 cup soft bread crumbs
1 lb cup mushrooms, sliced
2 zucchini, sliced
salt and pepper

one Put the dried mushrooms in a bowl, cover with boiling water, and leave to stand while preparing the remaining ingredients.

two Bring a large saucepan of water to a boil with 1 tablespoon of the oil. Add the pasta sheets, one at a time, and cook for about 4 mins until just tender. Drain.

three Meanwhile, mix together in a small bowl the mascarpone, garlic, dill or tarragon, and season to taste with salt and pepper. Melt half the butter in a frying pan. Add the bread crumbs, and fry gently for 2 mins. Drain on paper towels.

four Melt the remaining butter in the pan with the remaining oil. Add the fresh mushrooms and the zucchini, and fry for about 6 mins until golden. Drain the dried mushrooms, add to the pan, and fry for 1 min.

five Lay 4 pieces of lasagna, spaced slightly apart, in a shallow ovenproof dish. Spoon over a third of the vegetables, then a spoonful of the mascarpone mixture. Add another piece of lasagna to each stack and spoon over more vegetables, and mascarpone. Finally, add the remaining lasagna, vegetables, and mascarpone.

six Scatter with the fried bread crumbs and bake in a preheated oven, 400°F, for 6–8 mins until heated through.

goat cheese linguini with garlic and herb butter

preparation time **5 mins**
cooking time **7 mins**
total time **12 mins** serves **4**

10 oz firm goat cheese
1 lemon
5 tablespoons butter
2 tablespoons olive oil
3 shallots, finely chopped
2 garlic cloves, crushed
⅓ cup mixed chopped herbs, such as tarragon, chervil, parsley, and dill
3 tablespoons capers
10 oz fresh linguini or ½ lb dried linguini
salt and pepper

one Thickly slice the goat cheese and arrange on a lightly oiled, foil-lined broiler rack. Broil under a preheated hot broiler for about 2 mins until golden. Keep warm.
two Using a zester, pare peel strips from the lemon, then squeeze the juice.
three Melt the butter in a frying pan or sauté pan with the oil. Add the shallots and garlic, and fry gently for 3 mins. Stir in the herbs, capers, and lemon juice, and season to taste with salt and pepper.
four Cook the pasta in plenty of lightly salted boiling water for about 2 mins or until just tender. Drain lightly and return to the saucepan. Add the goat cheese and herb butter, and toss the ingredients together gently. Serve scattered with the strips of lemon peel.

stir-fried vegetable noodles

preparation time **10 mins**
cooking time **12 mins**
total time **22 mins** serves **4**

½ lb medium egg noodles
4 tablespoons peanut oil
1 bunch of scallions, sliced
2 carrots, thinly sliced
2 garlic cloves, crushed
¼ teaspoon dried chili flakes
¼ lb snow peas
¼ lb shiitake mushrooms, halved
3 Chinese leaves, shredded
2 tablespoons light soy sauce
3 tablespoons hoisin sauce

one Cook the noodles in lightly salted boiling water for about 4 mins or until just tender. Drain.
two Heat the oil in a large frying pan or wok. Add the scallions and carrots, and stir-fry for 3 mins. Add the garlic, chili flakes, snow peas, and mushrooms, and stir-fry for 2 mins. Add the Chinese leaves and stir-fry for 1 min.
three Add the drained noodles to the pan with the soy sauce and hoisin sauce. Stir-fry over a gentle heat for 2 mins until heated through. Serve immediately.

If you cannot get fresh pasta for this dish, use dried and cook
it while you make the sauce. Always lightly drain pasta so that
it retains plenty of moisture and does not dry out the sauce.

A single Thai chili gives this dish a really fiery kick.
Substitute a mild chili if you are feeling cautious!

vegetable noodles in spiced coconut milk

preparation time **10 mins**
cooking time **10 mins**
total time **20 mins** serves **4**

¼ lb dried medium egg noodles
2 tablespoons peanut or vegetable oil
1 onion, chopped
1 Thai chili, seeded and sliced
3 garlic cloves, sliced
2 inch piece of fresh ginger root, peeled
   and grated
2 teaspoons ground coriander
½ teaspoon ground turmeric
1 lemon grass stalk, finely sliced
14 oz can coconut milk
1¼ cups Vegetable Stock (see page 9)
1¼ cups finely shredded spring greens
   or cabbage
½ lb green beans sliced diagonally
2 cups sliced shiitake mushrooms
½ cup unsalted, shelled peanuts
salt and pepper

one Put the noodles in a bowl, cover with boiling water and leave to stand for 4 mins.
two Heat the oil in a large saucepan. Add the onion, chili, garlic, ginger, coriander, turmeric, and lemon grass, and fry gently for 5 mins.
three Drain the noodles. Add the coconut milk and stock to the pan and bring just to a boil. Reduce the heat and stir in the spring greens or cabbage, beans, mushrooms, and drained noodles. Cover and simmer for 5 mins. Stir in the peanuts and season to taste with salt and pepper. Serve in deep bowls.

rice noodles with green beans and ginger

preparation time **10 mins**
cooking time **5 mins**
total time **15 mins** serves **4**

¼ lb fine rice noodles
¼ lb green beans, halved
finely grated peel and juice of 2 limes
1 Thai chili, seeded and finely chopped
1 inch piece of fresh ginger root, peeled and
   finely chopped
2 teaspoons superfine sugar
small handful of cilantro, chopped
⅓ cup chopped, dried pineapple pieces

one Put the noodles in a bowl, cover with plenty of boiling water and leave for 4 mins until soft.
two Meanwhile, cook the beans in boiling water for about 3 mins until tender. Drain.
three Mix together the lime peel and juice, chili, ginger, superfine sugar, and cilantro in a small bowl.
four Drain the noodles and put in a large serving bowl. Add the cooked beans, pineapple, and dressing. Toss together lightly before serving. To make a chilled alternative, refresh the noodles and beans under cold running water. To turn the dish into a main course for 2, stir in some diced smoked tofu.

rice noodle pancakes with stir-fried vegetables

preparation time **15 mins**
cooking time **15 mins**
total time **30 mins** serves **4**

6 oz dried wide rice noodles
1 green chili, seeded and sliced
1 inch piece of fresh ginger root, peeled
 and grated
3 tablespoons chopped cilantro
2 teaspoons all-purpose flour
2 teaspoons oil, plus extra for shallow-frying

STIR-FRIED VEGETABLES
¼ lb broccoli
2 tablespoons peanut or vegetable oil
1 small onion, sliced
1 red bell pepper, cored, seeded and sliced
1 yellow or orange bell pepper, cored, seeded
 and sliced
¼ lb sugarsnap peas, halved lengthwise
6 tablespoons hoisin sauce
1 tablespoon lime juice
salt and pepper

one Cook the noodles in lightly salted boiling water for 3 mins or until tender. Drain well. Transfer to a bowl, then add the chili, ginger, cilantro, flour, and the 2 teaspoons of oil and mix well. Set aside.

two Thinly slice the broccoli stalks and cut the florets into small pieces. Cook the stalks in boiling water for 30 seconds. Add the florets and cook for 30 seconds more. Drain the broccoli well.

three Heat the peanut or vegetable oil in a wok or large frying pan, add the onion and stir-fry for 2 mins. Add the bell peppers and stir-fry for 3 mins until softened but still retaining texture. Stir in the cooked broccoli, sugarsnap peas, hoisin sauce, and lime juice. Season to taste with salt and pepper and set aside.

four Heat some oil in a frying pan to a depth of ½ inch. Put 4 large separate spoonfuls of the noodles (half the mixture) in the oil. Fry for about 5 mins until crisp and lightly colored. Drain the pancakes on paper towels. Keep warm while cooking the remaining noodle mixture.

five Heat the vegetables through for 1 min in the wok or frying pan. Put 2 pancakes on each of 4 serving plates and pile the stir-fried vegetables on top.

beans and pulses

Simply opening a can of beans, lentils, or other pulses provides the vegetarian cook with one of the most versatile vehicles for quick and easy main meals. Use them purely as a base ingredient, letting the highly flavored additions of garlic, spices, herbs, and aromatics transform them into culinary delights.

nut koftas with minted yogurt

preparation time **15 mins**
cooking time **10 mins**
total time **25 mins** serves **4**

5–6 tablespoons peanut or vegetable oil
1 onion, chopped
½ teaspoon crushed chili flakes
2 garlic cloves, roughly chopped
1 tablespoon medium curry paste
14 oz can borlotti or cannellini beans, rinsed
    and drained
1 cup ground almonds
¾ cup chopped honey-roast or salted almonds
1 small egg
1 cup Greek yogurt
2 tablespoons chopped mint
1 tablespoon lemon juice
salt and pepper
warm naan bread, to serve
mint sprigs, to garnish

one Soak 8 bamboo skewers in hot water while preparing the koftas. Alternatively, use metal skewers which do not require pre-soaking. Heat 3 tablespoons of the oil in a frying pan. Add the onion and fry for 4 mins. Add the chili flakes, garlic, and curry paste, and fry for 1 min.

two Transfer to a food processor or blender with the beans, ground almonds, chopped almonds, egg, and a little salt and pepper, and process until the mixture starts to bind together.

three Using lightly floured hands, take about one-eighth of the mixture and mold around a skewer, forming it into a sausage about 1 inch thick. Make 7 more koftas in the same way.

four Place on a foil-lined broiler rack and brush with 1 tablespoon of the oil. Broil under a preheated moderate broiler for about 5 mins, until golden, turning once.

five Meanwhile, mix together the yogurt and mint in a small serving bowl and season to taste with salt and pepper. In a separate bowl, mix together the remaining oil, lemon juice, and a little salt and pepper.

six Brush the koftas with the lemon dressing and serve with the yogurt dressing on warm naan bread garnished with mint sprigs.

braised lentils with mushrooms and gremolata

preparation time **5 mins**
cooking time **25 mins**
total time **30 mins** serves **4**

¼ cup butter
1 onion, chopped
2 celery sticks, sliced
2 carrots, sliced
1 cup Puy lentils, rinsed
2½ cups Vegetable Stock (see page 9)
1 cup dry white wine
2 bay leaves
2 tablespoons chopped thyme
3 tablespoons extra virgin olive oil
¾ lb mushrooms, sliced
salt and pepper

GREMOLATA
2 tablespoons chopped parsley
finely grated peel of 1 lemon
2 garlic cloves, chopped

one Melt the butter in a saucepan and fry the onion, celery, and carrots for 3 mins. Add the lentils, stock, wine, herbs, and a little salt and pepper. Bring to a boil, then reduce the heat and simmer gently, uncovered, for about 20 mins or until the lentils are tender.
two Meanwhile, mix together the ingredients for the gremolata.
three Heat the oil in a frying pan. Add the mushrooms and fry for about 2 mins until golden. Season lightly with salt and pepper.
four Ladle the lentils onto serving plates, top with the mushrooms, and serve scattered with the gremolata.

black bean and cabbage stew

preparation time **8 mins**
cooking time **20 mins**
total time **28 mins** serves **4**

4 tablespoons olive oil
1 large onion, chopped
1 leek, chopped
3 garlic cloves, sliced
1 tablespoon paprika
2 tablespoons chopped marjoram or thyme
1¼ lb potatoes, cut into small chunks
14 oz can black beans or black-eyed beans, rinsed and drained
4 cups Vegetable Stock (see page 9)
2 cups shredded cabbage or spring greens
salt and pepper
chunky bread, to serve

one Heat the oil in a large saucepan. Add the onion and leek, and fry gently for 3 mins. Add the garlic and paprika, and fry for 2 mins.
two Add the marjoram or thyme, potatoes, beans, and stock, and bring to a boil. Reduce the heat, cover and simmer gently for about 10 mins until the potatoes have softened but are not mushy.
three Add the cabbage or spring greens and season to taste with salt and pepper. Simmer for 5 mins more. Serve the stew with chunky bread.

red lentil dhal with okra

preparation time **5 mins**
cooking time **25 mins**
total time **30 mins** serves **4**

1 onion, chopped
½ lb red split lentils, rinsed and drained
1 teaspoon ground turmeric
1 green chili, seeded and sliced
2 tablespoons tomato paste
3¾ cups Vegetable Stock (see page 9)
2 tablespoons creamed coconut
2 tablespoons peanut or vegetable oil
½ lb okra, trimmed and halved crossways
2 teaspoons cumin seeds
1 tablespoon mustard seeds
2 teaspoons black onion seeds
2 garlic cloves, chopped
6 curry leaves (optional)
salt and pepper

one Put the onion, lentils, turmeric, chili, tomato paste, stock, and creamed coconut in a saucepan. Bring to a boil, then reduce the heat and simmer gently, uncovered, for 15 mins until the mixture is thickened and pulpy, stirring frequently.

two Meanwhile, heat the oil in a frying pan. Add the okra, cumin seeds, mustard seeds, black onion seeds, garlic, and curry leaves, if using, and fry gently for about 5 mins until the okra is tender.

three Season the lentil dhal to taste with salt and pepper, and spoon onto serving plates. Serve topped with the spiced okra.

Red lentils cook much faster than many pulses and do not need pre-soaking, making them a perfect choice for quick and easy cooking. Serve this spicy dish with naan or paratha bread and mango chutney to complete the meal.

chickpea puree with eggs and spiced oil

preparation time **5 mins**
cooking time **7 mins**
total time **12 mins** serves **2**

13 oz can chickpeas, rinsed and drained
3 garlic cloves, sliced
4 tablespoons tahini
4 tablespoons milk
5 tablespoons olive oil
4 teaspoons lemon juice
2 eggs
½ teaspoon each of cumin, coriander,
   and fennel seeds, lightly crushed
1 teaspoon sesame seeds
¼ teaspoon chili flakes
good pinch of ground turmeric
salt and pepper
cilantro leaves, to garnish

one Put the chickpeas in a food processor or blender with the garlic, tahini, milk, 2 tablespoons of the oil, and 3 teaspoons of the lemon juice. Season to taste with salt and pepper, and process until smooth, scraping the mixture from around the sides of the bowl halfway through. Transfer to a small heavy-based saucepan and heat through gently for about 3 mins while preparing the eggs.

two Heat another tablespoon of the oil in a small frying pan and fry the eggs. Pile the chickpea puree onto serving plates and top each mound with an egg.

three Add the remaining oil and spices to the pan and heat through gently for 1 min. Season lightly with salt and pepper, and stir in the remaining lemon juice. Pour over the eggs and serve garnished with cilantro leaves.

Smooth chickpea puree, topped with fried eggs and
spicy oil, makes a great snack at any time of the day.
Serve any leftover puree just as you would hummus,
with warm pita bread.

cannellini beans on toast

Preparation time **5 mins**
cooking time **25 mins**
total time **30 mins** serves **2–3**

2 tablespoons peanut or vegetable oil
1 onion, chopped
1 celery stick, thinly sliced
1 teaspoon cornstarch
14 oz can cannellini beans
1 cup canned chopped tomatoes
1¼ cups Vegetable Stock (see page 9)
1 tablespoon coarse-grain mustard
1 tablespoon dark corn syrup
1 tablespoon tomato ketchup
1 tablespoon Worcestershire sauce
salt and pepper
toasted chunky bread, to serve

one Heat the oil in a saucepan and fry the onion and celery for 5 mins until golden. Blend the cornstarch with 2 tablespoons water and add to the pan with the remaining ingredients.
two Bring to a boil, reduce the heat slightly and cook, uncovered, for about 20 mins, stirring frequently, until the mixture is thickened and pulpy. Pile on toast to serve.

red beans with coconut and cashews

preparation time **8 mins**
cooking time **22 mins**
total time **30 mins** serves **4**

3 tablespoons peanut or vegetable oil
2 onions, chopped
2 small carrots, thinly sliced
3 garlic cloves, crushed
1 red bell pepper, cored, seeded and chopped
2 bay leaves
1 tablespoon paprika
3 tablespoons tomato paste
14 fl oz can coconut milk
1 cup canned chopped tomatoes
⅔ cup Vegetable Stock (see page 9)
14 oz can red kidney beans, rinsed and drained
1 cup unsalted, shelled cashew nuts, toasted
small handful of cilantro, roughly chopped
salt and pepper
boiled black or white rice, to serve

one Heat the oil in a large saucepan. Add the onions and carrots, and fry for 3 mins. Add the garlic, pepper, and bay leaves, and fry for 5 mins until the vegetables are soft and well browned.
two Stir in the paprika, tomato paste, coconut milk, tomatoes, stock, and beans, and bring to a boil. Reduce the heat and simmer, uncovered, for 12 mins until the vegetables are tender.
three Stir in the cashew nuts and cilantro. Season to taste with salt and pepper and heat through for 2 mins. Serve with rice.

bean and beer casserole with baby dumplings

preparation time **5 mins**
cooking time **25 mins**
total time **30 mins** serves **4**

4 tablespoons peanut or vegetable oil
1 onion, sliced
1 celery stick, thinly sliced
1 parsnip, sliced
14 oz can mixed beans, rinsed and drained
14 oz can baked beans in tomato sauce
1 cup Guinness or stout
1 cup Vegetable Stock (see page 9)
4 tablespoons roughly chopped herbs, such
    as rosemary, marjoram, and thyme
1¼ cups self-rising flour
⅓ cup vegetable suet
2 tablespoons coarse-grain mustard
salt and pepper

one Heat the oil in a large saucepan
or flameproof casserole and fry the
onion, celery, and parsnip for 3 mins.
Add the mixed beans, baked beans,
beer, stock, and 3 tablespoons of the
herbs. Bring to a boil and let the mixture
bubble, uncovered, for 8–10 mins until
slightly thickened.
two Meanwhile, mix the flour, suet,
mustard, remaining herbs, and a little salt
and pepper in a bowl with 8–9 tablespoons
cold water to make a soft dough.
three Evenly distribute 8 spoonfuls of
the dough in the casserole and cover
with a lid. Cook for 10 mins more until
the dumplings are light and fluffy.
Serve immediately.

chili cheese and corn cakes

preparation time **15 mins**
cooking time **6 mins**
total time **21 mins** serves **4**

¾ cup frozen corn, thawed
7 oz can lima beans, rinsed
¾ cup semolina or polenta
1 cup grated cheddar cheese
½ teaspoon dried chili flakes
4 tablespoons mango chutney
1 egg
oil, for shallow-frying
salt and pepper

one Put the corn and beans in a food
processor or blender and process until
chopped into very small pieces, or mash
with a fork in a bowl. Transfer to a bowl, if
necessary, and add the semolina or polenta,
cheese, and chili flakes.
two Chop any large pieces of chutney. Add
to the bowl with the egg and mix to a dough.
Season with salt and pepper.
three Using lightly floured hands, shape
the mixture into 12 balls, then flatten into
cakes. Heat a little oil in a frying pan. Add
the cakes and fry gently for about 3 mins
on each side until golden. Drain and
serve warm.

red bean and bell pepper cakes with lemon mayonnaise

preparation time **10 mins**
cooking time **10 mins**
total time **20 mins** serves **4**

¾ cup roughly chopped green beans
2 tablespoons peanut or vegetable oil
1 red bell pepper, cored, seeded and diced
4 garlic cloves, crushed
2 teaspoons mild chili powder
14 oz can red kidney beans, rinsed and drained
1½ cups fresh white bread crumbs
1 egg yolk
oil, for shallow-frying
salt and pepper

LEMON MAYONNAISE
4 tablespoons mayonnaise
finely grated peel of 1 lemon
1 teaspoon lemon juice

one Blanch the green beans in boiling water for 1–2 mins until softened. Drain.

two Meanwhile, heat the peanut or vegetable oil in a frying pan. Add the red bell pepper, garlic, and chili powder, and fry for 2 mins.

three Transfer the mixture to a food processor or blender and add the red kidney beans, bread crumbs, and egg yolk. Process very briefly until the ingredients are coarsely chopped. Add the drained green beans and season to taste with salt and pepper, and process, again very briefly, until the ingredients are just combined.

four Put the mixture into a bowl and divide into 8 portions. Using lightly floured hands, shape the portions into little cakes.

five Mix the mayonnaise with the lemon peel and juice, and season to taste with salt and pepper.

six Heat the oil for shallow-frying in a large frying pan and fry the cakes for about 3 mins on each side until crisp and golden. Serve with the lemon mayonnaise.

Pack these crisp bean cakes into warm pita bread and serve with salad for a fairly substantial lunch or supper dish. Any unbaked cakes will keep in the refrigerator, interleaved with waxed paper, for a day or so.

rice

Rice is the staple ingredient of so many countries worldwide that it offers a fabulous choice of interesting dishes for the vegetarian cook. Although some varieties take longer to cook, there are still plenty of easy options on offer, including sweet, aromatic oriental dishes, spicy Middle Eastern-style pilafs, and creamy, comforting Italian risottos.

chestnut risotto cakes

preparation time **10 mins**
cooking time **20 mins**
total time **30 mins** serves **4**

1½ tablespoons dried bolete mushrooms
1 tablespoon olive oil
¾ cup risotto rice
2½ cups hot Vegetable Stock (see page 9)
¼ cup butter
1 onion, chopped
3 garlic cloves, crushed
1¼ cups cooked, peeled chestnuts
¾ cup grated Parmesan cheese
1 egg, lightly beaten
½ cup polenta
oil, for shallow-frying
salt and pepper

one Put the dried mushrooms in a bowl and cover with boiling water. Leave to stand.
two Heat the olive oil in a saucepan and cook the rice, stirring, for 1 min. Add the hot stock and bring to a boil. Reduce the heat, partially cover and simmer for 12–15 mins, stirring frequently, until the rice is tender and the stock is absorbed. Transfer to a bowl.
three Meanwhile, melt the butter in a saucepan. Add the onion and garlic, and fry gently for 2 mins. Drain and chop the mushrooms, then add to the rice with the onion mixture, chopped chestnuts, Parmesan, and egg. Stir until combined and season lightly with salt and pepper.
four Divide into 12 portions, pat each into a cake and coat in the polenta. Heat the oil for shallow-frying and fry the cakes for 2 mins on each side until golden. Serve immediately.

fava bean, lemon, and parmesan risotto

preparation time **5 mins**
cooking time **25 mins**
total time **30 mins** serves **4**

2 tablespoons butter
2 tablespoons olive oil
1 onion, chopped
2 garlic cloves, crushed
2 cups risotto rice
⅔ cup dry white wine
5 cups hot Vegetable Stock (see page 9)
1 cup fresh or frozen fava beans
½ cup grated Parmesan cheese, plus
    extra to serve
finely grated peel and juice of 1 lemon
salt and pepper

one Melt the butter with the oil in a large, heavy-based saucepan. Add the onion and garlic and fry gently for 3 mins. Add the rice and cook for 1 min, stirring.
two Add the wine and cook, stirring, until the wine is absorbed. Add a little stock and cook, stirring, until almost absorbed. Continue in the same way, gradually adding more stock, until half the stock is used. Stir in the beans.
three Gradually add the remaining stock until the mixture is thickened and creamy but still retaining a little bite. This will take 15–18 mins. Stir in the Parmesan, lemon peel and juice, and season to taste with salt and pepper. Transfer to serving plates and serve with extra Parmesan cheese.

red rice and bell pepper pilaf

preparation time **5 mins**
cooking time **25 mins**
total time **30 mins** serves **4**

1⅓ cups Camargue red rice
2½ cups hot Vegetable Stock (see page 9)
3 tablespoons olive oil
1 large red onion, chopped
2 tablespoons paprika
3 garlic cloves, crushed
1 teaspoon saffron threads
2 red bell peppers, cored, seeded and sliced
finely grated peel of 1 lemon
2 teaspoons lemon juice
4 tomatoes, roughly chopped
small handful of Italian parsley, roughly
    chopped, plus extra to garnish
⅓ cup pitted black olives
salt and pepper

one Put the rice, hot stock, and 2½ cups boiling water in a large saucepan. Bring to a boil, cover and cook for 25 mins until tender, stirring frequently.

two Meanwhile, heat the oil in a saucepan or sauté pan. Add the onion and fry gently for 3 mins. Add the paprika, garlic, saffron, and bell peppers, and fry gently for 5 mins.

three Stir in the lemon peel and juice, tomatoes, and parsley, and cook gently, uncovered, for 5 mins.

four Drain the rice and add to the pan with the olives. Season to taste with salt and pepper. Toss together and serve scattered with extra parsley.

japanese rice with nori

preparation time **10 mins**
cooking time **15 mins**
total time **25 mins** serves **4**

½ lb Japanese sushi or glutinous rice
2 tablespoons black or white sesame seeds
1 teaspoon coarse salt
1 tablespoon peanut or vegetable oil
2 eggs, beaten
4 scallions, finely sliced
1 red chili, seeded and sliced
4 tablespoons seasoned rice vinegar
2 teaspoons superfine sugar
1 tablespoon light soy sauce
2 tablespoons pickled Japanese ginger
2 sheets of roasted nori seaweed

one Put the rice in a heavy-based saucepan with 1⅔ cups water. Bring to a boil, then reduce the heat and simmer, uncovered, for about 5 mins until all the water is absorbed. Cover the pan and cook for 5 mins more until the rice is cooked.

two Meanwhile, put the sesame seeds in a small frying pan with the salt and heat gently for about 2 mins until the seeds are lightly toasted. Remove from the pan and set aside.

three Heat the oil in the pan. Add the beaten eggs and cook gently until just firm. Slide the omelet onto a plate, roll up and cut across into shreds.

four Transfer the cooked rice to a bowl and stir in the scallions, chili, rice vinegar, sugar, soy sauce, ginger, and half the toasted sesame seeds. Crumble 1 sheet of nori over the rice and stir in with the omelet shreds.

five Transfer to a serving dish. Crumble the remaining nori over the rice and scatter with the remaining toasted sesame seeds.

spiced pilaf with pickled walnuts

preparation time **7 mins**
cooking time **23 mins**
total time **30 mins** serves **4**

3 tablespoons olive oil
1 large onion, chopped
4 garlic cloves, sliced
¼ teaspoon ground allspice
½ cup pine nuts
2 teaspoons ground ginger
½ lb long-grain rice
1 teaspoon saffron threads
1¼ cups Vegetable Stock (see page 9)
½ cup roughly chopped pickled walnuts
⅓ cup sliced ready-to-eat dried apricots
4 tablespoons roughly chopped cilantro
salt and pepper
Greek yogurt, to serve

one Heat the oil in a large, heavy-based frying pan or sauté pan. Add the onion, garlic, allspice, pine nuts, and ginger, and fry gently for 5 mins.
two Add the rice and cook for 1 min, stirring. Add the saffron and stock, and bring to a boil. Reduce the heat, partially cover and simmer gently for 10–15 mins until the rice is tender, adding a little more stock if the mixture becomes too dry.
three Add the pickled walnuts, apricots, and cilantro. Season to taste with salt and pepper. Heat through for 2 mins, then serve with Greek yogurt.

sage and walnut risotto with a cheese crust

preparation time **5 mins**
cooking time **25 mins**
total time **30 mins** serves **4**

¼ cup butter
1 onion, chopped
¾ lb risotto rice
5¼ cups hot Vegetable Stock (see page 9)
2 tablespoons chopped sage
½ cup roughly chopped walnuts
½ lb Brie, thinly sliced
salt and pepper
leafy salad, to serve

one Melt the butter in a large, heavy-based saucepan. Add the onion and fry for 2 mins. Add the rice and fry for 1 min, stirring.
two Add 2 ladlefuls of the stock and cook, stirring, until almost absorbed. Add a little more stock and continue cooking, stirring, until almost absorbed. Continue in the same way until all the stock is used and the rice is creamy but still retaining a little bite. This will take 15–18 mins.
three Stir in the sage and walnuts, and season to taste with salt and pepper. Transfer to a shallow flameproof serving dish and cover with the slices of Brie. Cook under a preheated hot broiler for about 3 mins until the cheese has melted. Serve with a leafy salad.

kedgeree with artichokes and rosemary butter

preparation time **5 mins**
cooking time **15 mins**
total time **20 mins** serves **4**

½ lb basmati rice
¼ cup butter, melted
1 tablespoon chopped rosemary
1 tablespoon chopped chives
1 tablespoon lime juice
2 tablespoons olive oil
1 onion, chopped
1 teaspoon coriander seeds, crushed
1 teaspoon fennel seeds, crushed
14 oz can artichoke hearts, rinsed, drained,
    and halved
6 hard-boiled eggs, cut into wedges
salt and pepper
lime wedges, to garnish

one Cook the rice in plenty of lightly salted boiling water for about 10 mins or until it is just tender. Drain well.

two Meanwhile, mix together the melted butter, chopped herbs, and lime juice, and season with salt and pepper.

three Heat the oil in a frying pan. Add the onion and spices and fry gently for 5 mins. Add the rice to the pan with the artichoke hearts. Season to taste with salt and pepper and heat through gently for 1 min. Lightly stir in the eggs.

four Transfer to serving plates and pour over the herb butter. Serve garnished with lime wedges.

Cooking food in banana-leaf packages keeps its flavor and
moisture intact and makes an exotic presentation if you are
entertaining. If not, simply wrap the rice in nonstick parchment
paper or foil for heating through.

coconut rice with peanut sauce

preparation time **15 mins**
cooking time **12 mins**
total time **27 mins** serves **4**

1⅓ cups jasmine or Thai fragrant rice
⅓ cup creamed coconut
¹/₂ teaspoon dried chili flakes
1 teaspoon superfine sugar
small handful of cilantro, chopped
4 x 11 inch lengths of banana leaf, washed
1 lime
1 papaya, peeled, seeded and sliced
4 scallions, shredded lengthwise
¾ cup roasted, salted cashew nuts
salt and pepper

SAUCE
½ small onion, finely chopped
1 lemon grass stalk, finely sliced
4 tablespoons peanut butter
1 tablespoon dark muscovado sugar
2 tablespoons creamed coconut
2 tablespoons soy sauce

one Put the rice in a saucepan with the creamed coconut and 1⅓ cups water. Bring to a boil, then reduce the heat and simmer gently, stirring frequently, for about 5 mins until the water is almost absorbed and the mixture is creamy. Remove the pan from the heat and stir in the chili flakes, superfine sugar, and cilantro. Season to taste with salt and pepper.

two Spoon the mixture onto the centers of the banana leaves. Fold over the sides to enclose the rice, then tuck the ends under to form packages. Place on a baking sheet and bake in a preheated oven, 425°F, for about 5 mins until the leaves have browned.

three Meanwhile, put the ingredients for the sauce in a small saucepan and heat through gently until thickened, stirring the mixture frequently.

four Using a stripper, pare fine strips of peel from the lime. Cut away the remaining white skin and discard, then cut between the membranes to remove the segments.

five Open the packages and add the papaya, scallions, cashew nuts, and lime segments and peel. Serve with the sauce.

lemon rice with feta and chargrilled peppers

preparation time **5 mins**
cooking time **25 mins**
total time **30 mins** serves **4**

3 tablespoons olive oil
1 onion, sliced
3 garlic cloves, crushed
1 small lemon, sliced
1¾ cups long-grain rice
2½ cups Vegetable Stock (see page 9)
1 tablespoon chopped rosemary
1 large zucchini
2 red bell peppers, cored, seeded and
  cut into 8
1 yellow bell pepper, cored, seeded and
  cut into 8
½ lb feta cheese, diced
salt and pepper

one Heat 2 tablespoons of the oil in a saucepan. Add the onion and fry for 3 mins. Add the garlic and lemon slices and fry for 2 mins. Add the rice, stock, and rosemary, and bring to a boil. Reduce the heat slightly, partially cover and cook for about 15 mins until the rice is just tender and the stock is absorbed.

two Cut the zucchini diagonally into long thin slices. Heat the remaining oil in a large frying pan. Add the zucchini slices and bell peppers and cook for 5 mins until colored, turning the vegetables and pressing the peppers down onto the pan with a fish slice as they soften.

three Add the cooked vegetables to the rice and fold in with the feta. Season with salt and pepper. Heat through for 1 min before serving.

beet risotto with horseradish and mixed leaves

preparation time **5 mins**
cooking time **25 mins**
total time **30 mins** serves **4**

4 tablespoons olive oil
1 large red onion, chopped
3 garlic cloves, crushed
2 cups risotto rice
5⅔ cups hot Vegetable Stock (see page 9)
¾ lb cooked beet, finely diced
4 tablespoons roughly chopped dill
1–2 tablespoons freshly grated horseradish or
  1 tablespoon hot horseradish from a jar
½ cup salted macadamia nuts or almonds
salt and pepper
mixed salad leaves, to serve

one Heat the oil in a large, heavy-based saucepan. Add the onion and garlic, and fry gently for 3 mins. Add the rice and cook for 1 min, stirring.

two Add 2 ladlefuls of the hot stock and cook, stirring frequently, until almost absorbed. Continue in the same way until all the stock is used and the rice is creamy but still retaining a little bite. This will take about 20 mins.

three Stir in the beet, dill, horseradish, and nuts. Season to taste with salt and pepper and heat through gently for 1 min. Spoon the risotto onto plates and serve with mixed salad leaves.

This risotto makes an impressive main course for 4 people, but will also serve 6–8 as a colorful appetizer. If you can find fresh horseradish, use it in place of the bottled variety. The flavor is far superior, but beware of its heat intensity which can be anything from harmlessly mild to hot and fiery, depending on its freshness.

pizza and bread

Made using a quick and simple bread base, lavishly topped pizzas are surprisingly quick to prepare and create an enduringly appealing lunch or supper dish. Ready-made breads, both yeast-risen and flat, offer ultra-easy meal solutions, providing instant bases for a variety of exciting vegetarian fillings and toppings.

spinach, onion, and cream cheese pizza

preparation time **12 mins**
cooking time **15 mins**
total time **27 mins** serves **4**

2 cups self-rising flour
3 tablespoons olive oil
1 teaspoon salt

TOPPING
½ cup full-fat soft cheese
½ cup crème fraîche
2 teaspoons chopped rosemary
3 tablespoons olive oil
1 large onion, finely sliced
¾ lb young spinach
salt and pepper

one Grease a large baking sheet. Put the flour in a bowl with the oil and salt. Add 7 tablespoons water and mix to a soft dough, adding a little more water, a teaspoonful at a time, if the dough is too dry. Roll out on a floured surface into a round about 11 inches in diameter. Place the round on the prepared baking sheet and bake in a preheated oven, 450°F, for 5 mins until a crust has formed.

two For the topping, beat together the cream cheese, crème fraîche, rosemary, and a little salt and pepper.

three Heat the oil in a frying pan and fry the onion for 3–4 mins until softened. Add the spinach and a little salt and pepper and cook, stirring, for about 1 min until the spinach has just wilted.

four Pile the spinach onto the pizza base, spreading to within ½ inch of the edge. Put spoonfuls of the cheese mixture over the spinach. Bake for 8 mins more or until turning golden.

spinach and egg muffins with mustard hollandaise

preparation time **10 mins**
cooking time **8 mins**
total time **18 mins** serves **4**

½ lb baby spinach
plenty of freshly ground nutmeg
1 tablespoon lemon juice
2 egg yolks
1 tablespoon coarse-grain mustard
⅓ cup lightly salted butter, diced
4 English muffins, split
1 tablespoon vinegar
4 eggs

one Place the spinach and nutmeg in a saucepan and add 1 tablespoon water. Set aside while making the sauce.
two Put the lemon juice, egg yolks, and mustard in a heatproof bowl over a pan of gently simmering water. Whisk in the butter, a piece at a time, until the sauce is thickened and smooth. This takes about 5 mins. If the sauce becomes too thick, whisk in a tablespoonful of hot water. Keep the sauce over the simmering water until ready to use.
three Toast the muffins and keep warm. Put the vinegar in a saucepan with plenty of hot water, bring to a boil, and poach the eggs. Cover the spinach pan with a lid and cook for about 1 min until the spinach has wilted.
four Transfer the muffins to serving plates. Pile them up with the spinach, followed by the poached eggs and finally the sauce. Serve immediately.

goat cheese, onion, and pine nut bruschetta

preparation time **5 mins**
cooking time **10 mins**
total time **15 mins** serves **2**

5 tablespoons olive oil
1 small red onion, chopped
3 tablespoons pine nuts
4 slices ciabatta bread
1 garlic clove, crushed
2 tablespoons chopped Italian parsley
5 oz firm goat cheese, thinly sliced

one Heat 2 tablespoons of the oil in a frying pan. Add the onion, and pine nuts and fry for 3 mins until softened.
two Toast one side of the bread under a preheated moderate broiler until golden. Mix together the garlic, parsley, and remaining oil in a bowl. Turn the bread over and spread with the garlic mixture. Broil until pale golden.
three Lay the goat cheese and onion mixture over the toast, increase the heat, and broil for 2 mins more. Serve warm.

tomato, artichoke, and mozzarella pizza

preparation time **10 mins**
cooking time **20 mins**
total time **30 mins** serves **4**

2 cups self-rising flour
3 tablespoons oil
1 teaspoon salt
2 tablespoons sun-dried tomato paste

TOPPING
1 tablespoon sun-dried tomato paste
2 large, mild red or green chilies, halved
   and seeded
3 tablespoons chopped mixed herbs, such
   as parsley, oregano, rosemary, and chives
⅓ cup sun-dried tomatoes in oil, drained and
   sliced
¾ cup baby artichokes in oil, drained
2 plum tomatoes, cut into quarters
5 oz mozzarella cheese, sliced
½ cup black olives
salt and pepper

one Grease a large baking sheet. Put the flour in a bowl with the oil, salt, and sun-dried tomato paste. Add 7 tablespoons water and mix to a soft dough, adding a little more water if necessary.

two Roll out the dough on a lightly floured surface to a round about 11 inches in diameter. Place on the prepared baking sheet and bake in a preheated oven, 450°F, for 5 mins.

three For the topping, spread the pizza base to within ½ inch of the edge with the sun-dried tomato paste. Cut the chilies in half lengthwise again and scatter over the pizza with half the herbs, the sun-dried tomatoes, artichokes, tomatoes, cheese, and olives. Scatter the remaining herbs on top and season lightly with salt and pepper. Return to the oven and bake for 10–15 mins until the cheese has melted and the vegetables are beginning to color.

Homemade pizzas look and taste infinitely better than most store-bought ones and are certainly much better value for money. If you are unable to find the large, really mild chilies, use strips of red bell pepper instead or scatter the pizza with a finely sliced hot chili.

tortilla wraps with refried beans and cilantro relish

preparation time **5 mins**
cooking time **5 mins**
total time **10 mins** serves **2**

8 oz can refried beans
2 tablespoons chili sauce
2 red bell peppers, cored, seeded and
    finely chopped
4 scallions, finely sliced
1 teaspoon cumin seeds
finely grated peel and juice of 1 lime
1 teaspoon superfine sugar
1 tablespoon chopped cilantro
4 tortillas
salt and pepper

one Put the beans in a small saucepan with the chili sauce and heat through gently for 3 mins.
two Mix together in a bowl the bell peppers, scallions, cumin seeds, lime peel and juice, sugar, and cilantro. Season to taste with salt and pepper.
three Lightly toast the tortillas and spread with the refried beans. Spoon over the cilantro mixture and roll up the tortillas.

cheddar burgers with cucumber salsa

preparation time **10 mins**
cooking time **8 mins**
total time **18 mins** serves **4**

7 oz can lima beans, rinsed
1 onion, finely chopped
1 carrot, grated
1 cup grated mature cheddar cheese
2 cups bread crumbs
1 egg
1 teaspoon cumin seeds
oil, for shallow-frying
4 round French rolls
salt and pepper
salad, to serve

SALSA
½ small cucumber
2 tablespoons chopped cilantro
2 scallions, finely chopped
1 tablespoon lemon or lime juice
1 teaspoon superfine sugar

one Put the lima beans in a bowl and lightly mash with a fork. Add the onion, carrot, cheese, bread crumbs, egg, cumin seeds, and salt and pepper, and mix until evenly combined.
two Shape the mixture into 4 small flat cakes. Heat a little oil in a large frying pan and fry the burgers for about 8 mins, turning once, until crisp and golden.
three Meanwhile, for the salsa, halve the cucumber, scoop out the seeds and finely chop. Toss in a bowl with the cilantro, scallions, lemon or lime juice, sugar, and a little salt and pepper.
four Split the rolls and sandwich with the burgers and salsa. Serve with salad.

Sun-dried tomato pesto has all the vibrant flavor of the better-known basil version (see page 8), and serves equally as many uses. Try it spread onto pizzas, tossed with pasta or stirred into vegetable soups and stews.

toasted goat cheese with sun-dried tomato pesto

preparation time **10 mins**
cooking time **5 mins**
total time **15 mins** serves **4**

4 chunky slices of walnut or grainy bread
½ lb goat cheese
leafy salad, to serve

SUN-DRIED TOMATO PESTO
½ cup sun-dried tomatoes in oil, drained
4 tablespoons pine nuts
10 pitted black olives
2 garlic cloves, roughly chopped
5 tablespoons olive oil
¼ cup grated Parmesan cheese
salt and pepper

one To make the pesto, put the sun-dried tomatoes in a food processor or blender with the pine nuts, olives, and garlic. Process until chopped.

two With the motor running, add the oil in a thin, steady stream. When combined, transfer to a bowl and stir in the Parmesan cheese and salt and pepper.

three Toast one side of the bread under a preheated moderate broiler. Turn the bread over and top with the goat cheese. Increase the heat, and broil until the cheese is melting and golden. Transfer to serving plates and spoon over the pesto. Serve with a leafy salad.

tortillas with minted chili and eggplant yogurt

preparation time **10 mins**
cooking time **10 mins**
total time **20 mins** serves **2**

4 tablespoons olive oil
1 medium eggplant, thinly sliced
small handful of mint, chopped
small handful of parsley, chopped
2 tablespoons chopped chives
1 green chili, seeded and thinly sliced
1 cup Greek yogurt
2 tablespoons mayonnaise
2 large tortillas
3 inch length of cucumber, thinly sliced
salt and pepper
paprika, to garnish

one Heat the oil in a frying pan. Add the eggplant and fry for about 10 mins until golden. Drain and set aside to cool.

two Mix the herbs with the chili, yogurt, and mayonnaise in a bowl. Season to taste with salt and pepper.

three Arrange the fried eggplant slices over the tortillas and spread with the Greek yogurt mixture. Arrange the cucumber slices on top. Roll up each tortilla, sprinkle with paprika and serve.

pancakes
and pastries

Whether made from batter or vegetables, pancakes can be classic or inventive, taking on a main meal role with an eclectic mix of tempting toppings and fillings to suit your tastes and moods. Extend the variety by using ready-made pastries, such as mouth-wateringly crisp phyllo and rich, golden puff pastry, for great results in just a few minutes.

phyllo, pesto, and mozzarella packages

preparation time **10 mins**
cooking time **10 mins**
total time **20 mins** serves **4**

¼ lb phyllo pastry sheets
¼ cup butter, melted
3 tablespoons Sun-dried Tomato Pesto
  (see page 65)
½ lb mozzarella cheese, drained and sliced
½ cup grated Parmesan cheese
salt and pepper
leafy salad, to serve

one Cut the phyllo pastry into 16 x 6 inch squares. Lay 8 squares on the work surface and brush with a little melted butter. Cover each with a second square.

two Dot the pesto into the centers of the squares and spread slightly. Arrange the mozzarella and Parmesan over the pesto. Season lightly with salt and pepper.

three Bring two opposite sides of the pastry over the filling to enclose completely. Lightly brush with butter, then fold over the two open ends to make packages. Place on a baking sheet with the ends uppermost.

four Brush with the remaining butter (melt a little more if necessary) and bake in a preheated oven, 400°F, for about 10 mins until golden. Serve warm with a leafy salad.

camembert and shallot tarts

preparation time **10 mins**
cooking time **20 mins**
total time **30 mins** serves **4**

¼ cup butter
8 large shallots, each cut into 4 wedges
1 tablespoon chopped lemon thyme
¾ lb puff pastry
¼ lb Camembert cheese, sliced
salt and pepper

one Lightly grease a baking sheet and sprinkle with water. Melt the butter in a frying pan, add the shallots and gently fry for 5 mins until softened. Stir in the thyme.

two Roll out the pastry on a lightly floured surface to an 8 inch square and cut into 4 squares. Transfer to the prepared baking sheet. Using the tip of a sharp knife, make a shallow cut along each side of the squares, ½ inch from the edges, to form a rim.

three Spoon the shallots and thyme into the centers of the pastries. Bake in a preheated oven, 425°F, for 10 mins until well risen. Arrange the cheese over the shallots and return to the oven for 5 mins more. Serve warm.

zucchini pancakes with emmental and bell peppers

preparation time **10 mins**
cooking time **20 mins**
total time **30 mins** serves **6**

¾ lb zucchini
1½ cups all-purpose flour
3 eggs
⅓ cup butter, melted
½ cup milk
1 tablespoon chopped thyme
6 tablespoons olive oil
10 oz eggplant, cut into small chunks
2 small red onions, sliced
2 red bell peppers, cored, seeded and sliced
13 oz can chopped tomatoes
2 tablespoons balsamic vinegar
oil, for shallow-frying
10 oz Emmental cheese, thinly sliced
salt and pepper

These crisp little pancakes, topped with melting cheese and a ratatouille-style topping, make a thoroughly enjoyable appetizer, or increase the size of the pancakes and serve with a salad for a main course.

one Grate the zucchini in a large bowl. Beat together the flour, eggs, butter, milk, and thyme to make a smooth batter. Stir in the grated zucchini and season with salt and pepper.

two Heat the olive oil in a large, heavy-based saucepan or sauté pan. Add the eggplant and onions, and fry for about 5 mins until turning golden. Add the bell peppers and continue frying quickly for about 3 mins until the vegetables are lightly browned. Add the tomatoes, vinegar, and salt and pepper. Reduce the heat and simmer gently, uncovered, for 10 mins while preparing the pancakes.

three Heat a little oil in a large frying pan. Add a tablespoonful of the pancake mixture to one side of the pan and spread to about 4 inches. Add as many more spoonfuls of the batter as the pan will contain and fry for about 2 mins until golden on the underside. Turn the pancakes and cook for 2 mins more. Drain on paper towels and transfer to a broiler pan. Cook the remainder of the pancakes (the mixture should make 12 in total).

four Arrange the cheese slices over the pancakes and broil under a preheated hot broiler until the cheese is melting. Arrange 2 pancakes on each serving plate, overlapping them slightly. Pile the bell pepper sauce on top and serve warm.

cherry tomato tartlets with pesto crème fraîche

preparation time **10 mins**
cooking time **18 mins**
total time **28 mins** serves **4**

2 tablespoons extra virgin olive oil
1 onion, finely chopped
¾ lb cherry tomatoes
2 garlic cloves, crushed
3 tablespoons sun-dried tomato paste
¾ lb puff pastry
beaten egg, to glaze
⅔ cup crème fraîche
2 tablespoons Pesto (see page 8)
salt and pepper
basil leaves, to garnish

one Lightly grease a large baking sheet and sprinkle with water. Heat the oil in a frying pan. Add the onion and fry for about 3 mins until softened. Halve about half of the tomatoes. Remove the pan from the heat. Add the garlic and sun-dried tomato paste, then stir in all the tomatoes, turning until they are lightly coated in the sauce.

two Roll out the pastry on a lightly floured surface and cut out four 5 inch rounds using a cutter or small bowl as a guide. Transfer to the prepared baking sheet and make a shallow cut ½ inch from the edge of each round using the tip of a sharp knife, to form a rim. Brush the rims with beaten egg. Pile the tomato mixture onto the centers of the pastries, making sure the mixture stays within the rims.

three Bake the tartlets in a preheated oven, 425°F, for about 15 mins until the pastry is risen and golden.

four Meanwhile, lightly mix together the crème fraîche, pesto, and salt and pepper in a bowl so that the crème fraîche is streaked with the pesto.

five When cooked, transfer the tartlets to serving plates and spoon over the crème fraîche and pesto mixture. Serve scattered with basil leaves.

minted pea cake with mozzarella, tomato, and basil

preparation time **10 mins**
cooking time **16 mins**
total time **26 mins** serves **4**

1 lb potatoes
½ lb shelled peas
3 tablespoons chopped mint
1 egg, lightly beaten
10 oz mozzarella cheese, sliced
6 plum tomatoes, sliced
6 tablespoons extra virgin olive oil
1 tablespoon balsamic vinegar
small handful of basil leaves, shredded
¼ cup butter
salt and pepper

one Cut the potatoes into chunks and cook in lightly salted boiling water for about 8 mins until softened but still retaining their firm texture.

two Meanwhile, cook the peas in a separate pan of lightly salted boiling water for 2 mins. Drain the peas and put in a bowl, then mash with a fork until broken up. Coarsely grate the potatoes and add to the bowl with the mint, beaten egg, and salt and pepper. Mix together until evenly combined.

three Arrange alternate overlapping slices of the cheese and tomatoes in a shallow flameproof dish and season lightly with salt and pepper. Mix 5 tablespoons of the olive oil with the vinegar and basil for the dressing.

four Melt the butter with the remaining oil in a heavy-based frying pan. Add the potato and pea mixture, and pack down gently in an even layer. Fry over a moderate heat for about 5 mins until the underside looks crisp and golden when the edge is lifted with a flexible knife.

five To turn the pancake, invert it onto a baking sheet or flat plate, then slide it back into the pan and fry for 3 mins more. While it is cooking, broil the cheese and tomatoes under a preheated hot broiler until the cheese starts to melt.

six Cut the pancake into wedges and transfer to serving plates. Pile the cheese and tomatoes on top and spoon over the dressing.

tofu, cinnamon, and honey packages

preparation time **15 mins**
cooking time **15 mins**
total time **30 mins** serves **4**

¼ cup butter
2 onions, chopped
½ cup slivered almonds, lightly crushed
1 tablespoon clear honey
1 teaspoon ground cinnamon
7 oz tofu, drained and diced
5 oz phyllo pastry
salt and pepper

one Melt half of the butter in a frying pan. Add the onions and fry for 3 mins until softened. Stir in the almonds and fry for 2 mins until turning golden. Stir in the honey, cinnamon, and tofu, and season to taste with salt and pepper.
two Melt the remaining butter in a small saucepan. Cut out 16 x 7 inch squares from the phyllo pastry. Lay 8 squares on a work surface and brush with a little melted butter. Cover each with a second square placed at an angle to create a star shape. Pile the tofu mixture onto the centers of the squares.
three Brush the edges of the pastry with a little butter. Bring the edges up over the filling and pinch together to make bundles. Repeat with the remaining pastries. Transfer to a baking sheet and brush with the remaining butter.
four Bake in a preheated oven, 400°F, for about 10 mins until the pastry is golden. Serve warm.

These tasty chickpea cakes, traditionally rolled into little balls and deep fried, make a great veggie supper served simply with a fresh, Greek-style salad.

falafel cakes

preparation time **10 mins**
cooking time **10 mins**
total time **20 mins** serves **4**

13 oz can chickpeas, rinsed and drained
1 onion, roughly chopped
3 garlic cloves, roughly chopped
2 teaspoons cumin seeds
1 teaspoon mild chili powder
2 tablespoons chopped mint
3 tablespoons chopped cilantro
1 cup bread crumbs
oil, for shallow-frying
salt and pepper

one Put the chickpeas in a food processor or blender with the onion, garlic, spices, herbs, bread crumbs, and a little salt and pepper. Blend briefly to make a chunky paste.
two Take spoonfuls of the mixture and flatten into cakes. Heat a ½ inch depth of oil in a frying pan and fry half the falafel for about 3 mins, turning once until crisp and golden. Drain on paper towels and keep warm while cooking the remainder.

lemon grass and tofu nuggets with chili sauce

preparation time **10 mins**
cooking time **10 mins**
total time **20 mins** serves **4**

1 bunch of scallions
2 inch piece of fresh ginger root, peeled
   and chopped
2 lemon grass stalks, roughly chopped
small handful of cilantro
3 garlic cloves, roughly chopped
1 tablespoon superfine sugar
1 tablespoon light soy sauce
10 oz tofu, drained
1½ cups bread crumbs
1 egg
oil, for shallow-frying
salt and pepper

DIPPING SAUCE
1 tablespoon clear honey
2 tablespoons soy sauce
1 red chili, seeded and sliced
2 tablespoons orange juice

one Thinly slice 1 scallion and set aside.
Roughly chop the remainder and put in a
food processor with the ginger, lemon grass,
cilantro, and garlic. Process lightly until mixed
together and chopped but still chunky. Add
the sugar, soy sauce, tofu, bread crumbs,
egg, and salt and pepper and process until
just combined.

two Take spoonfuls of the mixture and pat
into flat cakes using lightly floured hands.

three Mix together the ingredients for the
dipping sauce, adding the reserved sliced
scallion, in a small serving bowl.

four Heat the oil in a large nonstick frying
pan. Add half the tofu cakes and fry gently
for 1–2 mins on each side until golden.
Drain on paper towels and keep warm
while frying the remainder. Serve with
the dipping sauce.

vegetable rice pancakes with sesame and ginger sauce

preparation time **15 mins**
cooking time **5 mins**
total time **20 mins** serves **4**

SAUCE
1 garlic clove, roughly chopped
2 inch piece fresh ginger root, peeled
   and roughly chopped
3 tablespoons light muscovado sugar
4 teaspoons soy sauce
5 teaspoons wine or rice vinegar
2 tablespoons tomato paste
2 tablespoons sesame seeds, plus extra
   to garnish

PANCAKES
8 rice pancakes
2 medium carrots
1 cup bean sprouts or mixed sprouting beans
small handful of mint, roughly chopped
1 celery stick, thinly sliced
4 scallions, thinly sliced diagonally
1 tablespoon soy sauce

one Put all the ingredients for the sauce, except the sesame seeds, in a food processor (use the small bowl of a food processor if you have one) or blender and process to a thin paste. Alternatively, crush the garlic, grate the ginger, and whisk with the remaining ingredients. Stir in the sesame seeds and transfer to a serving bowl.

two Soften the rice pancakes according to the packet directions. Cut the carrots into fine shreds and mix with the bean sprouts or sprouting beans, mint, celery, scallions, and soy sauce.

three Divide the vegetable mixture among the 8 pancakes and spoon into the middle of each. Fold in the bottom edge of each pancake to the middle, then roll up from one side to the other to form a pocket.

four Steam the pancakes in a vegetable steamer or bamboo steamer for about 5 mins until they are heated through. Alternatively, arrange on a wire rack set over a roasting pan of boiling water and cover with foil. Serve immediately with the sauce, garnished with sesame seeds.

Paper-thin rice pancakes make interesting wraps for a feast of tempting fillings—here, a light vegetable version. Served with a highly flavored sauce, they make an intriguing appetizer. Allow 2 rice pancakes per portion, but if there is a lot to follow, one is probably enough.

couscous, polenta, and grains

Couscous, polenta, bulghur wheat, and millet take their place among the seemingly ever-expanding range of cereal-based products that is now widely available. Each adds its own individual flavor and texture to vegetarian dishes, whether used as an integral ingredient or as a simple accompaniment.

couscous fritters with beets and crème fraîche

preparation time **15 mins**
cooking time **5 mins**
total time **20 mins** serves **4**

⅔ cup couscous
7 tablespoons hot Vegetable Stock (see page 9)
4 scallions, finely chopped
2 garlic cloves, chopped
3 tablespoons chopped parsley
¾ cup roughly chopped pine nuts
½ cup ground almonds
finely grated rind of 1 lemon
1 egg
oil, for frying
4 small cooked beets, cut into wedges
salt and pepper
Italian parsley, to garnish
crème fraîche, to serve

DRESSING
4 tablespoons extra virgin olive oil
1 teaspoon Tabasco sauce
1 tablespoon lemon juice

one Put two-thirds of the couscous in a bowl. Add the vegetable stock and leave to stand for 5 mins. Meanwhile, mix together the ingredients for the dressing in a small bowl.

two When the couscous has absorbed all the stock, fluff up with a fork and stir in the scallions, garlic, parsley, pine nuts, almonds, lemon peel, and egg. Season with salt and pepper and mix until the ingredients bind together.

three Take heaped teaspoonfuls of the mixture and shape into balls. Roll them in the remaining couscous, spread on a plate. Wet your hands before rolling the balls if the mixture starts to stick.

four Heat a 1 inch depth of oil in a sauté pan or heavy-based saucepan. Add the couscous balls to the oil, half at a time, and fry for about 2 mins until golden. Drain the first batch on paper towels while cooking the remainder.

five Arrange the beet wedges on serving plates and pile the fritters beside them. Top with a spoonful of crème fraîche, garnish with parsley, and serve with the dressing spooned over the top.

spiced vegetable couscous

preparation time **5 mins**
cooking time **25 mins**
total time **30 mins** serves **4**

½ lb couscous
4 tablespoons olive oil
1 large onion, chopped
3 garlic cloves, crushed
2 inch piece of fresh ginger root, peeled
    and grated
½ teaspoon dried chili flakes
2 teaspoons each of paprika and
    ground cumin
1 teaspoon ground turmeric
1 cinnamon stick, halved
1 medium sweet potato, diced
14 oz can chickpeas, rinsed
1¾ cups Vegetable Stock (see page 9)
½ cup raisins or golden raisins
salt and pepper
cilantro leaves, to garnish

one Put the couscous in a shallow
ovenproof dish, pour over 1¼ cups boiling
water and cover. Put in a preheated oven,
300°F, while preparing the vegetables.
two Heat the oil in a large saucepan. Add
the onion, garlic, ginger, and spices. Fry
gently, stirring, for 5 mins until golden.
three Add the sweet potato, chickpeas,
stock, and dried fruit. Season with salt and
pepper and bring to a boil. Reduce the heat,
cover and simmer for 20 mins until the
potatoes are tender.
four Fluff up the couscous with a fork and
spoon onto serving plates. Top with the
vegetables and sauce, and serve scattered
with cilantro leaves.

If you want to add extra flavor to the
polenta, stir in some fresh chopped
herbs, grated Parmesan, or a generous
pat of butter.

soft polenta with gruyère and tomato sauce

preparation time **10 mins**
cooking time **20 mins**
total time **30 mins** serves **4**

½ lb instant polenta
3 garlic cloves, chopped
4 tablespoons olive oil
1 large onion, chopped
13 oz can chopped tomatoes
3 tablespoons sun-dried tomato paste
2 teaspoons light muscovado sugar
¾ cup grated Gruyère or cheddar cheese
salt and pepper

one Bring 4 cups water to a boil in a large
saucepan with 1 teaspoon salt. Add the
polenta in a steady stream, then the garlic,
and cook, stirring, for 5 mins until the
polenta is very thick and pulpy. Transfer to
a lightly greased shallow ovenproof dish.
two Heat the oil in a saucepan. Add the
onion and fry for 5 mins. Add the tomatoes,
sun-dried tomato paste, and sugar to the
onion. Season to taste with salt and pepper.
Spoon the mixture over the polenta.
three Scatter with the grated cheese and
bake in a preheated oven, 400°F, for 10 mins
until golden.

green couscous with spiced fruit sauce

preparation time **10 mins**
cooking time **15 mins**
total time **25 mins** serves **4**

½ lb couscous
2 cups hot Vegetable Stock (see page 9)
¾ cup unsalted, shelled pistachio nuts,
    roughly chopped
2 scallions, chopped
small handful of parsley, chopped
14 oz can flageolet beans, rinsed and drained
½ teaspoon saffron threads
1 tablespoon cardamom pods
2 teaspoons coriander seeds
½ teaspoon chili powder
4 tablespoons slivered almonds
⅔ cup ready-to-eat dried apricots
salt and pepper

To reveal their stunning emerald green color, pistachio nuts are best skinned by immersing them in boiling water for one minute, then rubbing off the skins between sheets of paper towels. Only do this if you have time since it is very labor-intensive!

one Put the couscous in a bowl. Add 1¼ cups of the hot stock. Leave to stand for 5 mins until the stock is absorbed, then stir in the pistachio nuts, scallions, parsley and beans. Season to taste with salt and pepper. Cover the bowl and put in a preheated oven, 300°F, for 15 mins.

two Meanwhile, put the saffron in a small cup with 1 tablespoon boiling water and leave for 3 mins. Crush the cardamom pods using a mortar and pestle, or put the pods in a small bowl and crush with the end of a rolling pin. Pick out and discard the pods, then lightly crush the seeds.

three Transfer to a food processor or blender with the coriander seeds, chili powder, almonds, and apricots. Process until finely chopped. Add the saffron and soaking liquid, the remaining stock, and salt and pepper and blend until pulpy. Transfer to a saucepan and heat through for 1 min. Serve with the couscous.

An abundance of herbs gives this salad its wonderful flavor. If prunes are not your favorite dried fruit, substitute just about any other—apricots, plump golden raisins or raisins. Figs and dates are also good in this recipe.

tabbouleh with fruit and nuts

preparation time **10 mins**, plus soaking
total time **25 mins** serves **4**

1¼ cups bulghur wheat
¾ cup unsalted, shelled pistachio nuts
1 small red onion, finely chopped
3 garlic cloves, crushed
2 tablespoons chopped Italian parsley
1½ tablespoons chopped mint
finely grated peel and juice of 1 lemon
    or lime
1 cup sliced ready-to-eat prunes
4 tablespoons olive oil
salt and pepper

one Put the bulghur wheat in a bowl, cover with plenty of boiling water, and leave to soak for 15 mins.
two Meanwhile, put the pistachio nuts in a separate bowl and cover with boiling water. Leave to stand for 1 min, then drain. Rub the nuts between several thicknesses of paper towels to remove most of the skins, then peel away any remaining skins with the fingers.
three Mix the nuts with the onion, garlic, parsley, mint, lemon or lime peel and juice, and prunes in a large bowl.
four Drain the bulghur wheat thoroughly in a sieve, pressing out as much moisture as possible with the back of a spoon. Add to the other ingredients with the oil and toss together. Season to taste with salt and pepper and chill until ready to serve.

mushroom, couscous, and herb sausages

preparation time **15 mins**
cooking time **10 mins**
total time **25 mins** serves **4**

⅓ cup couscous
3 tablespoons olive oil
1 onion, chopped
½ lb chestnut mushrooms, roughly chopped
1 red chili, seeded and finely sliced
3 garlic cloves, roughly chopped
small handful of mixed herbs, such as thyme,
    rosemary, and parsley
1½ cups whole cooked chestnuts
1½ cups bread crumbs
1 egg yolk
oil, for shallow-frying
salt and pepper

one Put the couscous in a bowl. Add 5 tablespoons boiling water and leave to stand for 5 mins.
two Meanwhile, heat the olive oil in a frying pan. Add the onion, mushrooms, and chili and fry quickly for about 5 mins until the mushrooms are golden and the moisture has evaporated.
three Transfer to a food processor or blender with the garlic, herbs, and chestnuts, and process until finely chopped. Transfer to a bowl and add the soaked couscous, bread crumbs, egg yolk, and salt and pepper.
four Using lightly floured hands, shape the mixture into 12 sausage shapes. Heat the oil for shallow-frying and fry the sausages for about 5 mins, turning frequently.

Millet is a small, golden grain that looks a little like couscous, and makes a perfect alternative to rice. Add some drained, canned lentils and a spoonful of harissa paste to turn this dish into a main course.

spiced millet

preparation time **5 mins**
cooking time **25 mins**
total time **30 mins** serves **4**

¼ cup butter
1 onion, chopped
2 garlic cloves, crushed
1 tablespoon cardamom pods, lightly crushed
2 teaspoons whole cloves
1 cinnamon stick, halved
1¾ cups millet
2½ cups Vegetable Stock (see page 9)
4 tablespoons chopped parsley
salt and pepper

one Melt the butter in a heavy-based saucepan. Add the onion and fry gently for 3 mins. Add the garlic, cardamom pods, cloves, cinnamon, and millet. Season to taste with salt and pepper and fry for 2 mins.
two Add the stock and the parsley, and bring to a boil. Reduce the heat and simmer gently, uncovered, for about 20 mins until the millet is tender and the stock absorbed. Lightly fork up the millet a couple of times during cooking to keep the grains light and separate. Serve hot.

polenta chips with saffron mushrooms

preparation time **10 mins**
cooking time **20 mins**
total time **30 mins** serves **4**

1 teaspoon saffron threads
1 lb ready-cooked polenta
1 tablespoon all-purpose flour
2 teaspoons chili powder
oil, for shallow-frying
2 tablespoons butter
1 onion, chopped
2 garlic cloves, crushed
¾ lb mixed wild and cultivated mushrooms, halved if large
½ lb mascarpone cheese
2 tablespoons chopped tarragon
finely grated peel and juice of ½ lemon
salt and pepper

one Put the saffron in a bowl with 1 tablespoon boiling water and leave to stand.
two Cut the polenta into ½ inch slices, then cut the slices into ½ inch chips. Mix together the flour, chili powder, and salt and pepper and use to coat the polenta.
three Heat a ½ inch depth of oil in a frying pan and fry the chips, half at a time, for about 10 mins until golden. Once cooked, drain on paper towels and keep warm.
four Meanwhile, melt the butter in a separate frying pan, add the onion and garlic, and fry for 5 mins. Stir in the mushrooms and fry for 2 mins. Add the mascarpone, tarragon, lemon peel and juice, saffron and soaking liquid, and season with salt and pepper. Stir until the mascarpone has melted to make a sauce. Serve with the polenta chips.

Unless you have the time to cook and set homemade polenta,
use a pack of ready-cooked polenta to make these chips.
Tossed in chili powder and shallow-fried, they make a
welcome change to the more traditional French fries.

salads and side salads

Creativity is the key when it comes to salads, composing with several carefully selected complementary ingredients to create a feast of color, flavor, and texture. Some of the salads presented are sufficiently sustaining to serve as main courses, while others make attractive appetizers or imaginative side dishes.

ribboned carrot salad

preparation time **10 mins**, plus soaking
total time **25–30 mins** serves **4**

4 medium carrots
2 celery sticks
1 bunch of scallions
4 tablespoons light olive oil
2 tablespoons lime juice
2 teaspoons superfine sugar
¼ teaspoon crushed dried chilies
2 tablespoons chopped mint
½ cup salted peanuts
salt and pepper

one Half fill a medium bowl with very cold
water, adding a few ice cubes if necessary.
two Scrub the carrots and pare off as many
long ribbons as you can from each. Put the
ribbons in the water. Cut the celery into
2 inch lengths. Cut each length into very
thin slices. Cut the scallions into 2 inch
lengths and shred lengthwise. Add the
celery and scallions to the water and leave
for 15–20 mins until the vegetables curl up.
three Mix together the oil, lime juice, sugar,
chilies, and mint in a small bowl and season
to taste with salt and pepper.
four Thoroughly drain the vegetables and
toss in a salad bowl with the dressing,
peanuts, and salt and pepper. Serve the
salad immediately.

sweet potato, arugula, and haloumi salad

preparation time **10 mins**
cooking time **15 mins**
total time **25 mins** serves **4**

1 lb sweet potatoes, sliced
3 tablespoons olive oil
½ lb haloumi cheese, patted dry on
    paper towels
1 cup arugula

DRESSING
5 tablespoons olive oil
3 tablespoons clear honey
2 tablespoons lemon or lime juice
1½ teaspoons black onion seeds
1 red chili, seeded and finely sliced
2 teaspoons chopped lemon thyme
salt and pepper

one Mix together all the ingredients for
the dressing in a small bowl.
two Cook the sweet potatoes in lightly
salted boiling water for 2 mins. Drain well.
Heat the oil in a large frying pan. Add the
sweet potatoes and fry for about 10 mins,
turning once, until golden.
three Meanwhile, thinly slice the cheese
and place on a lightly oiled foil-lined broiler
rack. Cook under a preheated moderate
broiler for about 3 mins until golden.
four Pile the sweet potatoes, cheese, and
arugula onto serving plates and spoon over
the dressing.

This combination of firm, salty cheese, sweet potato, and a honeyed, spiced citrus dressing is absolutely delicious. This quantity serves 4 as a light lunch or supper dish, or 6 as an appetizer.

broiled baby eggplant and tomato salad

preparation time **10 mins**
cooking time **10 mins**
total time **20 mins** serves **4**

½ lb baby eggplants
4 tablespoons olive oil
1 tablespoon lemon juice
2 tablespoons roughly chopped chervil
   or parsley
½ lb cherry tomatoes, halved
1 teaspoon superfine sugar
2 garlic cloves, crushed
7 oz ricotta cheese
⅔ cup arugula
4 teaspoons balsamic vinegar
salt and pepper

Serve this colorful salad either as an appetizer for 4 or a more substantial supper for 2. Although appealing, baby eggplants are not always available, so substitute a large eggplant, thickly sliced, if you cannot find any.

one Halve the eggplants and cut criss-cross lines over the cut surfaces for decoration. Put, cut sides up, on a foil-lined broiler rack and drizzle with 1 tablespoon of the oil, the lemon juice, and salt and pepper. Broil under a preheated hot broiler for 8–10 mins, turning once, until the slices are tender and golden, then sprinkle them with the chervil or parsley.

two Meanwhile, put the tomatoes in a frying pan with another tablespoon of the oil and sprinkle with the sugar, garlic, and salt and pepper. Fry quickly for 1–2 mins until softened but not mushy.

three Arrange the eggplants on warmed serving plates. Pile the ricotta, then the tomatoes and finally the arugula on top. Add the balsamic vinegar, the remaining oil, salt and pepper, and any juices on the foil to the frying pan and heat through for 30 seconds. Pour over the salad before serving.

thai-dressed tofu rolls

preparation time **10 mins**
total time **10 mins** serves **4**

1 small iceberg lettuce
2 cups diced tofu
¼ lb snow peas, shredded lengthwise
2 tablespoons sesame oil
2 tablespoons light soy sauce
2 tablespoons lime juice
1 tablespoon muscovado sugar
1 Thai chili, seeded and sliced
1 garlic clove, crushed
pepper

one Remove 8 leaves from the lettuce. Fill a large heatproof bowl with boiling water. Add the separated leaves and leave for 10 seconds. Rinse in cold water and drain thoroughly.
two Finely shred the remaining lettuce and toss in a bowl with the tofu and snow peas.
three Mix together the sesame oil, soy sauce, lime juice, sugar, chili, garlic, and pepper, and add to the tofu mixture. Toss together gently, using 2 spoons.
four Spoon a little mixture onto the center of each blanched lettuce leaf, then roll up. Chill until ready to serve.

beet salad with cilantro and tomato salsa

preparation time **10 mins**
total time **10 mins** serves **4**

8 medium cooked beets, sliced
2 tablespoons red wine vinegar
1 teaspoon superfine sugar
2 tablespoons light olive oil
salt and pepper
crème fraîche, to serve
cilantro sprigs, to garnish

SALSA
1 red onion, finely chopped
¾ lb small vine-ripened tomatoes, seeded
    and chopped
2 garlic cloves, crushed
1½ tablespoons chopped cilantro

one Toss the beets in a bowl with the vinegar, sugar, oil, and salt and pepper.
two Mix together the ingredients for the salsa in a separate bowl. Season lightly with salt and pepper.
three Arrange about two-thirds of the beet slices on 4 serving plates. Pile the salsa onto the beets, then add the remaining beet slices. Top with spoonfuls of crème fraîche and spoon over any dressing left in the beet bowl. Serve garnished with cilantro sprigs.

spiced orange and avocado salad

preparation time **10 mins**
total time **10 mins** serves **4**

4 large juicy oranges
2 small ripe avocados, pitted and peeled
2 teaspoons cardamom pods
3 tablespoons light olive oil
1 tablespoon clear honey
good pinch of ground allspice
2 teaspoons lemon juice
salt and pepper
watercress sprigs, to garnish

This refreshing, summery side salad can easily be transformed into a main course with the addition of diced smoked tofu or goat cheese. Serve with a grainy, malty bread.

one Cut the skin and the white membrane off the oranges. Working over a bowl to catch the juice, cut between the membranes to remove the segments.
two Slice the avocados and toss gently with the orange segments. Pile onto serving plates.
three Reserve a few whole cardamom pods for garnish. Crush the remaining pods using a mortar and pestle to extract the seeds, or put in a small bowl and crush with the end of a rolling pin. Pick out and discard the pods. Mix the seeds with the oil, honey, allspice, lemon juice, salt and pepper, and reserved orange juice.
four Garnish the salads with the watercress sprigs and serve with the dressing spooned over the top.

herb salad with stem ginger and grapes

preparation time **5 mins**
total time **5 mins** serves **4**

1 small fennel bulb, finely chopped
½ lb seedless white grapes, halved
2 pieces of bottled stem ginger, finely chopped
2 tablespoons syrup from the ginger jar
4 tablespoons grape or apple juice
2 tablespoons olive oil
3 cups mixed herb or leaf salad greens
½ cup unsalted cashews or walnuts (optional)
salt and pepper

one In a medium bowl, mix together the fennel, grapes, ginger and ginger syrup, fruit juice, and oil. Season to taste with salt and pepper.
two Put the salad leaves in a serving bowl and add the nuts, if using. Add the other ingredients and toss together lightly before serving.

potato and green bean salad

preparation time **10 mins**
cooking time **15 mins**
total time **25 mins** serves **4**

1¾ lb new potatoes, scrubbed
1½ cups green beans, halved
6 tablespoons extra virgin olive oil
4 teaspoons lemon juice
2 teaspoons pink peppercorns
1 teaspoon superfine sugar
4 tablespoons chopped chives
4 eggs
salt and pepper
watercress or sorrel, to serve

one Cook the potatoes in plenty of lightly salted boiling water for about 15 mins or until just tender.

two Meanwhile, cook the green beans in a separate pan of boiling water for 2–3 mins until just tender. Drain and refresh under cold water.

three Mix together the oil, lemon juice, peppercorns, sugar, chives, and salt and pepper in a bowl.

four Lower the eggs into a small saucepan of boiling water and cook for 4 mins. (Cook the eggs for an extra 3 mins if you prefer them hard-boiled.) Drain.

five Drain the potatoes, then immerse in a bowl of water to cool. Drain. Shell and quarter the eggs.

six Toss the potatoes, green beans and eggs in the dressing. Pile onto a bed of watercress or sorrel on individual serving plates.

panzanella

preparation time **15 mins**
cooking time **10 mins**
total time **25 mins** serves **4**

3 red bell peppers, cored, seeded
  and quartered
¾ lb ripe plum tomatoes, peeled
6 tablespoons extra virgin olive oil
3 tablespoons wine vinegar
2 garlic cloves, crushed
½ stale ciabatta bread roll
⅓ cup pitted black olives
small handful of basil leaves, shredded
salt and pepper

one Place the bell peppers, skin side up, on a foil-lined broiler rack and broil under a preheated moderate broiler for 10 mins or until the skins are blackened.

two Meanwhile, quarter the tomatoes and scoop out the pulp, putting it in a sieve over a bowl to catch the juices. Set the tomato quarters aside. Press the pulp with the back of a spoon to extract as much juice as possible.

three Beat the oil, vinegar, garlic, and salt and pepper into the tomato juice.

four When cool enough to handle, peel the skins from the bell peppers and discard. Roughly slice the bell peppers and put in a bowl with the tomato quarters. Break the bread into small chunks and add to the bowl with the olives and basil.

five Add the dressing and toss the ingredients together before serving.

In this classic Italian salad, pieces of ciabatta bread are tossed with the other ingredients, absorbing the wonderful flavor of the garlicky tomato dressing. It is best to use slightly stale ciabatta which will not fall apart. Alternatively, use lightly toasted fresh bread. This quantity serves 4 as an appetizer or 2 as a main course.

vegetable dishes

Vegetarian cooking thrives on the amazing array of exotic, seasonal, and everyday vegetables that we can now easily find, and the many different ways in which they can be cooked. Here, fresh herbs, fragrant spices, and other subtle seasonings are used to bring out the essential flavors of the ingredients to create delicious main meals, snacks, and accompaniments.

deviled mushrooms on brioche

preparation time **5 mins**
cooking time **7 mins**
total time **12 mins** serves **2**

4 teaspoons mango chutney
¾ inch piece of fresh ginger root, peeled
  and grated
2 tablespoons Worcestershire sauce
1 tablespoon coarse-grain mustard
2 teaspoons paprika
5 tablespoons fresh orange juice
2 brioche buns or 2 large slices of brioche
2 tablespoons butter
1 tablespoon oil
3 shallots, thinly sliced
½ lb chestnut mushrooms, halved
2 tablespoons sour cream

one Cut up any large pieces of mango
and mix the chutney with the ginger,
Worcestershire sauce, mustard, paprika,
and orange juice.
two Thickly slice the buns, if using, and
toast the brioche. Keep warm.
three Melt the butter in a frying pan with the
oil. Add the shallots and fry gently for 3 mins
until softened. Add the mushrooms and fry
quickly for about 3 min, stirring, until golden.
four Add the chutney mixture to the pan
and heat through for 1 min, then stir in the
cream. Spoon over the toasted brioche and
serve hot.

celeriac and potato remoulade with asparagus

preparation time **10 mins**
cooking time **7 mins**
total time **17 mins** serves **4**

1 lb celeriac, peeled
¾ lb potatoes, peeled
1 tablespoon extra virgin olive oil,
  plus extra for drizzling (optional)
1 lb asparagus, trimmed

SAUCE
⅔ cup mayonnaise
⅔ cup Greek yogurt
1 teaspoon Dijon mustard
6 cocktail gherkins, finely chopped
2 tablespoons capers, chopped
2 tablespoons chopped tarragon
salt and pepper

one Cut the celeriac and potato into
matchstick-size pieces, but keep the two
vegetables separate. Cook the celeriac in
lightly salted boiling water for 2 mins until
softened. Add the potatoes and cook for
2 mins more until just tender. Drain the
vegetables and refresh under running water.
two Meanwhile, mix together the
ingredients for the sauce and set aside.
three Heat the oil in a frying pan or griddle
pan. Add the asparagus and fry for 2–3 mins
until just beginning to color.
four Mix the celeriac and potato with the
sauce and spoon onto 4 serving plates. Top
with the asparagus stalks.
five Serve immediately, drizzled with a little
extra olive oil, if desired.

To make this summery lunch or supper dish
more substantial, lightly poach some eggs
and arrange them over the asparagus.

wilted spinach with pine nuts and raisins

preparation time **5 mins**
cooking time **2 mins**
total time **7 mins** serves **4**

¼ cup plump raisins
3 tablespoons olive oil
⅓ cup pine nuts
2 garlic cloves, crushed
1½ lb baby spinach
finely grated peel of 1 lemon
salt and pepper

one Put the raisins in a small bowl, cover with boiling water and leave for 5 mins.
two Meanwhile, heat the oil in a large frying pan or sauté pan and fry the pine nuts until pale golden. Stir in the garlic.
three Thoroughly drain the raisins and add to the pan with the spinach. Cook for about 1 min, turning the ingredients together until the spinach has just wilted. Add the lemon peel, season to taste with salt and pepper, and serve immediately.

This refreshing combination of flavors makes a good accompaniment to pizza, bean, or pasta dishes, or serve as a light tapas on its own to excite the appetite.

deep-fried zucchini with minted yogurt

preparation time **10 mins**
cooking time **10 mins**
total time **20 mins** serves **4**

3 medium zucchini
1 small onion, very thinly sliced
1 egg
½ teaspoon medium curry paste
1 cup all-purpose flour
oil, for deep-frying

MINTED YOGURT
7 tablespoons Greek yogurt
2 tablespoons chopped mint

one Coarsely grate the zucchini and mix in a bowl with the onion.
two In a separate bowl, beat the egg with the curry paste and 7 tablespoons cold water. Whisk in the flour. Add the zucchini and onions, and mix until evenly combined.
three Mix the yogurt with the mint in a small serving dish.
four Heat a 2 inch depth of oil in a deep-fat fryer or large, heavy-based saucepan until a drop of the batter sizzles and rises to the surface. Add heaped spoonfuls of the batter to the pan and fry for about 3 mins until crisp and golden. Drain on paper towels and keep warm while cooking the remainder. You will probably need to fry the batter in 3 batches. Serve with the minted yogurt.

mushroom toad-in-the-hole with beer and onion gravy

preparation time **5 mins**
cooking time **25 mins**
total time **30 mins** serves **4**

4 large Portobello mushrooms,
   or ¾ lb smaller open mushrooms
2 tablespoons butter
5 tablespoons olive oil
3 garlic cloves, sliced
2 tablespoons chopped rosemary
   or thyme
1 cup all-purpose flour
2 eggs
2 tablespoons hot horseradish sauce
1⅔ cups milk
2 onions, sliced
2 teaspoons superfine sugar
1 cup stout
⅔ cup Vegetable Stock (see page 9)
salt and pepper

one Put the mushrooms, stalk sides up, in a large shallow ovenproof dish. Melt the butter with 4 tablespoons of the oil in a frying pan. Add the garlic and herbs. Season to taste with salt and pepper, and stir for 30 seconds. Pour the mixture over the mushrooms. Bake in a preheated oven, 450°F, for 2 mins.

two Meanwhile, blend the flour, eggs, horseradish, milk, and a little salt in a food processor or blender until smooth. Alternatively, put the flour in a bowl and gradually whisk in the eggs, horseradish, milk, and a little salt.

three Pour the batter over the mushrooms and bake for 20–25 mins until the batter is well risen and golden.

four Meanwhile, heat the remaining oil in a frying pan. Add the onions and sugar, and fry for about 5 mins until deep golden. Add the beer and stock, and season to taste with salt and pepper. Cook, stirring frequently, for 5 mins. Serve poured over the mushroom batter.

baby squash with red bean sauce

preparation time **10 mins**
cooking time **15 mins**
total time **25 mins** serves **4**

2½ cups Vegetable Stock (see page 9)
2 lb mixed baby squash, such as gem,
    butternut, or acorn
¼ lb baby spinach

SAUCE
4 tablespoons olive oil
4 garlic cloves, thinly sliced
1 red bell pepper, cored, seeded and
    finely chopped
2 tomatoes, chopped
14 oz can red kidney beans, rinsed and drained
1–2 tablespoons hot chili sauce
small handful of cilantro, chopped
salt

TO SERVE
steamed white rice
sour cream (optional)
avocado and lime salad (optional)

one Bring the stock to a boil in a large saucepan. Quarter and seed the squash. Add to the pan, reduce the heat and cover. Simmer gently for about 15 mins or until the squash are just tender.

two Meanwhile, to make the sauce, heat the oil in a frying pan, add the garlic and bell pepper, and fry for 5 mins, stirring frequently, until very soft. Add the tomatoes, red kidney beans, chili sauce, and a little salt, and simmer for 5 mins until pulpy.

three Drain the squash from the stock, reserving the stock, and return to the pan. Scatter over the spinach leaves, cover and cook for about 1 min until the spinach has wilted in the steam.

four Pile the vegetables onto steamed rice on serving plates. Stir 8 tablespoons of the reserved stock into the sauce with the cilantro. Spoon over the vegetables and serve with sour cream and an avocado and lime salad if desired.

This is a great dish to make during the fall, when various baby squash and pumpkin are at their most plentiful.

A frittata is an Italian-style omelet and, like an omelet, can be flavored in many interesting ways. For best results, use a good-quality, heavy-based, frying pan and really fresh, flavorsome eggs.

watercress and mushroom frittata

preparation time **5 mins**
cooking time **15 mins**
total time **20 mins** serves **3–4**

6 eggs
5 tablespoons grated Parmesan cheese
1 bunch of watercress, tough stalks removed
3 tablespoons butter
½ lb mushrooms, thinly sliced
salt and pepper

one Beat the eggs in a bowl with a fork to break them up. Stir in the Parmesan, watercress, and plenty of salt and pepper.
two Melt the butter in a heavy-based frying pan. Add the mushrooms and fry quickly for 3 mins. Pour in the egg mixture and gently stir the ingredients together.
three Reduce the heat to its lowest setting and fry gently until the mixture is lightly set and the underside is golden when the edge of the frittata is lifted with a flexible knife. If the base of the frittata starts to catch before the top is set, put it under a moderate broiler to finish cooking.

basil and tomato stew

preparation time **10 mins**
cooking time **15 mins**
total time **25 mins** serves **4**

2 lb ripe tomatoes, peeled
6 tablespoons olive oil
2 onions, chopped
4 celery sticks, sliced
4 plump garlic cloves, thinly sliced
6 oz mushrooms, sliced
3 tablespoons sun-dried tomato paste
2½ cups Vegetable Stock (see page 9)
1 tablespoon muscovado sugar
3 tablespoons capers
large handful of basil leaves
large handful of chervil or Italian parsley
salt and pepper
warm bread, to serve

one Quarter and seed the tomatoes, scooping out the pulp into a sieve over a bowl to catch the juices.
two Heat 4 tablespoons of the oil in a large saucepan and fry the onions and celery for 5 mins. Add the garlic and mushrooms, and fry for 3 mins more.
three Add the tomatoes and their juices, sun-dried tomato paste, stock, sugar, and capers, and bring to a boil. Reduce the heat and simmer gently, with the pan uncovered, for 5 mins.
four Tear the herbs into pieces, add to the pan with a little salt and pepper, and cook for 1 min. Ladle into bowls, drizzle with the remaining oil, and serve with warm bread.

spaghetti squash with cabbage and nuts

Preparation time **10 mins**
Cooking time **20 mins**
Total time **30 mins** Serves **3–4**

1 spaghetti squash, weighing about 3 lb
3 tablespoons butter
1 onion, thinly sliced
2 garlic cloves, crushed
5 oz finely shredded green cabbage
¾ cup natural peanuts or cashews
¼ cup crème fraîche
plenty of freshly grated nutmeg
salt and pepper

one Put the squash in a large pan in which it just fits. Cover with boiling water and boil for 20 mins.

two Meanwhile, melt the butter in a frying pan and gently fry the onion and garlic for 5 mins. Stir in the cabbage and fry for 3 mins until tender. Add the nuts, crème fraîche, and nutmeg. Season to taste with salt and pepper, and cook until the crème fraîche melts to make a sauce.

three Drain and halve the spaghetti squash, and discard the seeds from the center. Using 2 forks, shred the flesh into a bowl, breaking it up into fine threads. Add to the frying pan and toss the ingredients together over the heat for 1 min. Serve immediately.

baked vine tomatoes with garlic and herbs

preparation time **5 mins**
cooking time **20 mins**
total time **25 mins** serves **4**

1 lb vine-ripened tomatoes
2 plump garlic cloves, thinly sliced
1 tablespoon roughly chopped thyme
   or rosemary
2 red chilies, halved lengthwise
5 tablespoons extra virgin olive oil
4 tablespoons balsamic vinegar
salt and pepper

one Cut the tomatoes from the vine in clumps of 2 or 3. Make a deep slit in each tomato and insert a couple of garlic slices, a good pinch of herbs, and season to taste with salt and pepper. Pack into a shallow ovenproof dish.

two Tuck the chili halves around the tomatoes. Pour over the oil and vinegar, and check the seasoning: you may need a little more salt and pepper. Bake in a preheated oven, 425°F, for 20 mins until the tomatoes are softened but not falling apart.

eggplant pâté

preparation time **10 mins**
cooking time **15 mins**
total time **25 mins** serves **6**

2 tablespoons dried bolete mushrooms
1 lb eggplants
6 tablespoons olive oil
1 small red onion, chopped
2 teaspoons cumin seeds
6 oz cup or chestnut mushrooms
2 garlic cloves, crushed
3 pickled walnuts, halved
small handful of cilantro
salt and pepper
toasted walnut or grainy bread, to serve

one Put the dried mushrooms in a bowl and cover with plenty of boiling water. Leave to soak for 10 mins.

two Meanwhile, cut the eggplants into $\frac{1}{2}$ inch dice. Heat the oil in a large frying pan. Add the eggplants and onion and fry gently for 8 mins until the vegetables are softened and browned.

three Drain the dried mushrooms and add to the pan with the cumin seeds, fresh mushrooms, and garlic. Fry for 5–7 mins more until the eggplants are very soft.

four Transfer to a food processor or blender with the pickled walnuts and cilantro. Season to taste with salt and pepper and process until broken up but not completely smooth. Transfer to a serving dish and serve warm or cold with toast.

Just a few dried mushrooms really boost the flavor of this quick and easy pâté. It makes plenty and leftovers keep well in the refrigerator for several days, ready for either zipping up vegetable stews or spreading onto toast and broiling with Gruyère cheese.

buttered cauliflower crumble

preparation time **8 mins**
cooking time **12 mins**
total time **20 mins** serves **4**

1 large cauliflower
2 tablespoons butter
1 cup bread crumbs
2 tablespoons olive oil
3 tablespoons capers
3 cocktail gherkins, finely chopped
3 tablespoons chopped dill or tarragon
¼ cup crème fraîche
4 tablespoons grated Parmesan cheese
salt and pepper

vegetable crisps

preparation time **10 mins**
cooking time **5 mins**
total time **15 mins** serves **4–6**

½ lb each potato, parsnip, and raw beets
oil, for deep-frying
coarse sea salt and pepper

one Cut the vegetables into very thin slices using the slicer attachment of a food processor or a mandoline. They can also be sliced by hand, although it can be difficult to get them sufficiently fine. Pat the vegetables dry on paper towels.
two Pour the oil into a deep-fat fryer or heavy-based saucepan until about a third full. Heat the oil until a piece of vegetable sizzles on the surface. Add a batch of vegetable slices to the oil and fry until crisp and golden. Drain on paper towels while frying the remainder. Serve generously seasoned with salt and pepper.

one Cut the cauliflower into large florets and blanch in boiling water for 2 mins. Drain the florets thoroughly.
two Melt half of the butter in a large frying pan. Add the bread crumbs and fry for 2 mins until golden. Drain and set aside.
three Melt the remaining butter in the pan with the oil. Add the cauliflower florets and fry gently for about 5 mins until golden. Add the capers, gherkins, dill or tarragon, and crème fraîche. Season to taste with salt and pepper and stir the mixture over a moderate heat for 1 min.
four Put the mixture into a shallow flameproof dish and sprinkle with the fried bread crumbs and Parmesan. Cook under a preheated moderate broiler for about 2 mins until the crumbs are dark golden brown.

pan-fried roots with cardamom and honey

preparation time **10 mins**
cooking time **15 mins**
total time **25 mins** serves **4**

½ lb small turnips, cut into wedges
1 small sweet potato, scrubbed and cut
    into chunks
½ lb medium parsnips, cut into wedges
8 shallots, peeled but left whole
1 tablespoon cardamom pods
2 tablespoons clear honey
2 teaspoons lemon juice
4 tablespoons olive oil
salt and pepper

one Cook the turnips, sweet potato, parsnips, and shallots in lightly salted boiling water for 7–8 mins until they are softened but not tender.

two Meanwhile, crush the cardamom pods using a mortar and pestle to release the seeds. Alternatively, crush the pods in a small bowl using the end of a rolling pin. Pick out and discard the pods, then pound the seeds to crush them slightly. Mix the crushed seeds with the honey, lemon juice, and a little salt and pepper.

three Drain the vegetables. Heat the oil in a large frying pan. Add the vegetables and fry for about 6 mins until golden, stirring frequently. Add the cardamom dressing and toss together for 1 min. Serve hot.

Crushed cardamom seeds are delicious with root vegetables, bringing out their sweet, earthy flavors. Serve as an accompaniment to vegetable pancakes and spicy rice and bean dishes.

desserts
and bakes

Simple cooking techniques such as pan-frying, baking, and broiling capitalize on the many winning qualities of fresh, ripe fruits to create irresistible desserts with the minimum of time and fuss. Bakes, too, can be quick as well as rewarding to make, providing a ready supply of luxurious snacks and indulgent sweet treats.

cranberry, oatmeal, and cinnamon scones

preparation time **10 mins**
cooking time **12 mins**
total time **22 mins** makes **10**

1½ cups self-rising flour
1 teaspoon baking powder
1 teaspoon ground cinnamon
5 tablespoons unsalted butter
5 tablespoons superfine sugar
½ cup oatmeal, plus extra for sprinkling
¾ cup dried cranberries
5–6 tablespoons milk
beaten egg or milk, to glaze

one Grease a baking sheet. Put the flour, baking powder, and cinnamon in a food processor. Add the butter, cut into small pieces, and process until the mixture resembles bread crumbs. Add the sugar and oatmeal, and blend briefly. Alternatively, use your fingertips to rub the butter into the flour, baking powder, and cinnamon in a bowl, then add the sugar and oatmeal.

two Add the cranberries and milk, and blend briefly until the mixture forms a soft dough, adding a little more milk if necessary.

three Put the mixture on a floured surface and roll out to ¾ inch thick. Cut out rounds using a 2 inch cutter. Transfer to the prepared baking sheet and re-roll the trimmings to make more scones.

four Brush with beaten egg or milk and sprinkle with oatmeal. Bake in a preheated oven, 425°F, for 10–12 mins until risen and golden. Transfer to a wire rack to cool. Serve split and buttered.

Like all scones, these sweet fruit-specked ones are best served freshly baked, or frozen ahead and then thawed and warmed through to serve.

This unbelievably easy dessert is perfect for any occasion, whether you are entertaining friends or are in desperate need of something sweet and delicious.

plum and amaretto tartlets

preparation time **10 mins**
cooking time **15 mins**
total time **25 mins** serves **6**

¾ lb puff pastry
a little beaten egg, to glaze
6 oz white or golden almond paste
confectioners' sugar, for dusting
1 lb red or yellow plums, halved and pitted
4 tablespoons Amaretto liqueur or brandy
lightly whipped cream, to serve

one Lightly grease a baking sheet and sprinkle with water. Roll out the pastry on a lightly floured surface and cut out six 4 inch rounds using a cutter or small saucer as a guide. Using the tip of a sharp knife, make a shallow cut ½ inch from the edge of each round to form a rim. Brush the tops with beaten egg and transfer to the baking sheet.
two Roll out the almond paste on a surface dusted with confectioners' sugar and cut out six 3 inch rounds. Place a round in the center of each tartlet. Arrange the plum halves over the almond paste, cut sides up, and drizzle with as much liqueur or brandy as the cavities will hold. Bake in a preheated oven, 425°F, for about 15 mins until the pastry is well risen.
three Spoon over any remaining liqueur and dust with confectioners' sugar. Serve the tartlets with whipped cream.

chunky oat cookies

preparation time **10 mins**
cooking time **15 mins**
total time **25 mins** makes **15**

½ cup unsalted butter, softened
½ cup golden superfine sugar
1 egg
2 teaspoons vanilla extract
1 cup porridge oats
4 tablespoons sunflower seeds
1¼ cups all-purpose flour
½ teaspoon baking powder
6 squares white chocolate, chopped
   into small pieces
confectioners' sugar, for dusting

one Lightly grease a large baking sheet.
Beat together the butter and sugar in a bowl
until creamy. Add the egg, vanilla, oats,
sunflower seeds, flour, and baking powder,
and mix together to make a thick paste. Stir
in the chocolate pieces.
two Place medium spoonfuls of the mixture
on the prepared baking sheet and flatten
slightly with the back of a fork.
three Bake in a preheated oven, 350°F, for
about 15 mins until risen and golden. Leave
for 5 mins, then transfer to a wire rack to
cool. Serve dusted with confectioners' sugar.

Use good-quality white chocolate
without the oversweet, cloying taste
of cheaper chocolate, or use milk or
dark chocolate if preferred.

quick tiramisu

preparation time **15 mins**, plus chilling
total time **15 mins** serves **4–6**

5 tablespoons strong espresso coffee
½ cup dark muscovado sugar
4 tablespoons coffee liqueur or
   3 tablespoons brandy
6–8 sponge finger cookies, broken into
   large pieces
1⅔ cups good-quality ready-made custard
½ lb mascarpone cheese
1 teaspoon vanilla extract
2 squares dark chocolate, finely chopped
cocoa powder, for dusting

one Mix the coffee with 2 tablespoons
of the sugar and the liqueur or brandy in
a medium bowl. Toss the sponge fingers
in the mixture and put into a serving dish,
spooning over any excess liquid.
two Beat together the custard, mascarpone,
and vanilla, and spoon a third over the
biscuits. Sprinkle with the remaining sugar,
then half the remaining custard. Scatter with
the chopped chocolate, then spread with the
remaining custard.
three Chill for about 1 hour until set. Serve
dusted with cocoa powder.

pan-fried apricots with gingered mascarpone

preparation time **5 mins**
cooking time **3 mins**
total time **8 mins** serves **4**

2 pieces of bottled stem ginger
2 tablespoons syrup from the ginger jar
½ lb mascarpone cheese
2 teaspoons lemon juice
¼ cup unsalted butter
2 tablespoons light muscovado sugar
¾ lb fresh apricots, halved
3 tablespoons Amaretto liqueur or brandy

one Finely chop the stem ginger and mix with the ginger syrup, mascarpone, and lemon juice.
two Melt the butter in a frying pan and add the sugar. Cook for about 1 min until the sugar has dissolved. Add the apricots and fry quickly until lightly colored but still firm. Stir in the liqueur or brandy.
three Spoon the mascarpone onto serving plates, top with the fruit and juices, and serve the dessert warm.

broiled peaches with brown sugar brûlée

preparation time **5 mins**
cooking time **5 mins**
total time **10 mins** serves **4**

4 large juicy peaches
⅔ cup heavy cream
2 teaspoons lemon juice
3 tablespoons unrefined confectioners' sugar
1 tablespoon slivered almonds

one Halve the peaches, remove the pits, and place, skin sides down, in a shallow flameproof dish.
two Mix the cream with the lemon juice and 1 tablespoon of the confectioners' sugar. Pour over the peaches. Sprinkle with the remaining confectioners' sugar, then the almonds.
three Cook under a preheated moderate broiler for about 5 mins until the sugar is bubbling and lightly caramelized. Serve warm.

A simple dessert that makes the most of fresh apricots during their all-too-short season. When they are not available, it is equally good made with red or yellow plums. Amaretti cookies make a no-fuss accompaniment.

toffee apple bake

preparation time **10 mins**
cooking time **20 mins**
total time **30 mins** serves **4**

3 eating apples, cored and thickly sliced
1 cup self-rising flour, plus 1 tablespoon extra
½ cup light muscovado sugar
¼ cup superfine sugar
½ teaspoon ground mixed spice
1 egg
7 tablespoons natural bio yogurt
¼ cup unsalted butter, melted

one Toss the apples in a shallow ovenproof dish with 1 tablespoonful of the flour and the muscovado sugar.
two Mix the remaining flour with the superfine sugar and spice in a bowl. Add the egg, yogurt, and butter, and stir lightly until only just combined.
three Spoon the mixture over the prepared apples and bake in a preheated oven, 425°F, for about 15–20 mins until just firm and golden. Serve warm.

A great standby that few can resist! During cooking, the muscovado sugar melts to form a deliciously smooth, toffee-like sauce for the apples. It is perfect served with vanilla ice cream.

blueberry and vanilla muffins

preparation time **5 mins**
cooking time **15 mins**
total time **20 mins** makes **10**

1½ cups ground almonds
⅔ cup golden superfine sugar
½ cup self-rising flour
¾ cup unsalted butter, melted
4 egg whites
1 teaspoon vanilla extract
1 cup blueberries

one Line 10 sections of a muffin pan with paper cases, or grease the sections. Mix together the ground almonds, sugar, flour, and butter. Add the egg whites and vanilla extract, and mix to a smooth paste.
two Spoon into the cases and scatter with the blueberries.
three Bake in a preheated oven, 425°F, for 15 mins until just firm in the center. Leave for 5 mins, then transfer the muffins to a wire rack to cool.

You need luscious, full-flavored eating pears, which
will soften quickly in the syrup, to make this dessert.

syrupy pears with chocolate crumble

preparation time **5 mins**
cooking time **8 mins**
total time **13 mins** serves **4**

¼ cup light muscovado sugar
3 tablespoons raisins
½ teaspoon ground cinnamon
4 ripe eating pears, peeled, halved, and cored
3 tablespoons unsalted butter
½ cup porridge oats
3 tablespoons roughly chopped hazelnuts
2 squares dark or milk chocolate, chopped
lightly whipped cream or Greek yogurt,
    to serve (optional)

one Put half of the sugar in a frying pan
or wide sauté pan with ⅔ cup water and
the raisins and cinnamon. Bring just to a
boil, add the pears, and simmer gently,
uncovered, for about 5 mins until the
pears are slightly softened.
two Melt the butter in a separate frying
pan or saucepan. Add the porridge oats
and fry gently for 2 mins. Stir in the
remaining sugar and cook over a gentle
heat until golden.
three Spoon the pears onto serving plates.
Stir the hazelnuts and chocolate into the oats
mixture. When the chocolate starts to melt,
spoon over the pears. Serve topped with
whipped cream or Greek yogurt if desired.

chocolate cherry slices

preparation time **10 mins**
total time **10 mins** serves **4**

14 oz can black cherries in syrup
3 tablespoons Kirsch
1 tablespoon lemon juice
¼ lb ricotta cheese
2 tablespoons confectioners' sugar
1 square dark chocolate, chopped
1 piece of bottled stem ginger, finely chopped
4 thick slices of moist chocolate cake

one Thoroughly drain the cherries,
reserving the syrup. Blend 4 tablespoons of
the syrup with the Kirsch and lemon juice.
two Mix together the ricotta and
confectioners' sugar in a bowl. Gently
fold in the cherries, chocolate, and ginger.
three Put the slices of chocolate cake on
serving plates and spoon over the Kirsch
syrup. Pile the cherry mixture on top.

Bought chocolate cake can be
dramatically transformed when bathed in
liqueured syrup and topped with cherries,
ricotta, and chocolate chunks.

Index

Acknowledgments

Executive Editor: Sarah Ford
Project Editor: Alice Tyler
Executive Art Editor: Geoff Fennell
Designer: Sue Michniewicz

Photographer: William Reavell
Stylist: Clare Hunt
Home Economist: Joanna Farrow
Production Controller: Ian Paton